The Compassionate Writer: Find Your Voice, Enhance Your Story, and Touch Lives

Anne E. Beall, PhD

THE COMPASSIONATE WRITER: FIND YOUR VOICE, ENHANCE YOUR STORY, AND TOUCH LIVES

Copyright © 2025 Anne E. Beall

All rights reserved. No part of this book may be reproduced in any form or by any electronic or mechanical means, including information storage and retrieval systems, without permission in writing from the author. The only exception is by a reviewer, who may quote short excerpts in a review.

Cover designed by Atiq Ahmed

ISBN: 979-8-9901929-2-8 (Paperback)
ISBN: 979-8-9901929-3-5 (Hard Cover)
ISBN: 979-8-9901929-4-2 (E-Pub)

To all writers who feel discouraged and question whether they'll ever be a "real writer," know this: if you are putting pen to paper or fingers to a keyboard, if words are finding their way onto the page, you are already a writer in every true sense of the word.

Contents

Introduction: Writing with Compassion 1

Chapter 1: Yes, You Have a Story 8

Chapter 2: The Inner Critic 20

Chapter 3: Self-Compassion and Embracing Vulnerability 35

Chapter 4: From Memory to Meaning: Turning Life into Story 55

Chapter 5: Writing Real People in Memoir: Balancing Truth with Empathy 76

Chapter 6: Creating Complex Characters in Fiction Through Empathy 101

Chapter 7: Writing Conflict with Compassion 119

Chapter 8: Emotional Journeys: How to Craft Stories that Touch the Heart 136

Chapter 9: Avoiding Exploitative or Harmful Narratives 159

Chapter 10: Writing to Heal: How Compassion Transforms Both Writer and Reader 176

Chapter 11: Overcoming Writer's Block with Compassion 196

Chapter 12: Compassionate Editing: Balancing Criticism and Kindness 212

Chapter 13: Cultivating a Compassionate Writing Community 229

Chapter 14: Rejection and Resilience: Using Compassion to Keep Going 245

Conclusion: The Compassionate Writer's Journey 262

Acknowledgements 268
Sources 270
About the Author 274

Introduction: Writing with Compassion

My Journey to Compassionate Writing

I didn't set out to become more compassionate—I just wanted to become a better writer. But along the way, I discovered that compassion wasn't just a nice quality to have; it was essential. I began to see how deeply it shaped my writing—and how much of a difference it made. This is my journey.

In my early work, especially when I told personal stories, I tended to simplify people. There was always a villain, always a victim. Sometimes I cast myself as the bad guy; other times, I was the one who'd been wronged. The people around me became exaggerated—saints or adversaries, but rarely the complex, contradictory humans they truly were.

I wasn't doing it on purpose—I was just trying to make sense of my experiences. But the result was writing that felt more like fairy tales than real life. It lacked emotional depth and wasn't entirely truthful.

The writing wasn't landing. The rejections piled up. My stories weren't going anywhere. So I joined critique groups, hoping to figure out what I was missing. The feedback I got was surprisingly consistent.

After one piece, someone said gently, "You're really hard on yourself in this." Another added, "The people in this story feel either awful or perfect. Were they really like that—or is that how it felt at the time?" Then someone looked at me and said, "I want to connect with the narrator—but it feels like she's hiding. Like we're getting a version of her, not the real person."

The Compassionate Writer

At first, I bristled. I wanted to argue. I thought I was being honest. But later, when I re-read the pieces, I saw what they meant. The facts weren't wrong, but the tone was unforgiving. I held everyone to a rigid standard, especially myself. I wanted to assign blame, to draw clear lines around what had happened. I tended to see things in absolutes.

So I started revisiting those memories—and those people—with more compassion. Instead of judging them, I asked: *What was really going on? What was I missing? Could I understand—not excuse, but truly understand—the people in these stories, including myself?* That shift changed everything.

My characters became more nuanced. My voice felt more honest. I leaned into the grey—the contradictions, the tensions, the messy, ordinary complexity of real life. I wasn't writing to prove something anymore. I was writing to understand.

At the same time, I began exploring compassion more intentionally in other areas of my life. That exploration led me to write *Embracing Compassion: Meditation Journeys for Self-Kindness*, a book of guided visualizations to help people soften their inner critic. It grew out of the same realization I was having in my writing: that self-judgment gets in the way of truth.

Eventually, I began leading workshops based on this perspective—helping writers revisit difficult memories. They wrote about a person who disappointed them, a time they felt ashamed, and then they rewrote those moments through a lens of compassion. The results were powerful. Writers uncovered emotional truths they hadn't seen before. Characters became more complex. Long-held pain began to loosen its grip. They were shifting from judgment to understanding. Participants told me they felt better—not just in their writing, but in their lives.

I also realized that the writing I admired most held a compassionate lens toward self and others. These authors didn't reduce themselves to villains or victims; they explored what it means to be human. As the founder of *Chicago Story Press*, I've read thousands of submissions. The stories I have published weren't necessarily the most dramatic or polished—they were the ones that felt true, the ones that explored the complexity of people and life. They needed compassion to do that.

It's humbling to admit that I hold a PhD in social psychology and am familiar with the research on compassion, but didn't realize I deserved it. And I didn't think my characters did, either. But we all do. I realized that we're all trying to find happiness in imperfect ways. We make mistakes. We hurt others. We fail. But my job as a writer isn't to lay blame—it's to understand.

What Compassion Looks Like in My Writing Life

I now try to have compassion for all parts of my writing process. And that starts with seeing my own value as a writer—even if I haven't published much, even if I don't have an MFA, even if I haven't been writing for thirty years. It begins with the belief that I have a story to tell, and that it matters.

It also means being kind to myself during the process—not beating myself up on the fallow days. Some days, the words come easily. Other days, they don't. I've learned not to measure my worth as a writer by word count. Writing is not a performance; it requires patience, care, and trust.

The Compassionate Writer

Compassion gives me permission to take my time and really listen for what the story wants to be. I've learned that clarity often takes time. I can let things sit for days, weeks, even months—and when I return, the story often reveals itself. By being gentle with myself and letting the story unfold on its own timeline, I've produced better work.

Whether I'm writing memoir or fiction, I try to meet myself where I am—with regrets and pride, failure and grace. I don't have to tell everything. But I tell the emotional truth I'm ready to face. That truth is what makes the work feel real.

Compassion has also transformed how I write about others—both real people and fictional characters. In some earlier work, I wrote from a place of anger and blame. But now I ask: *What shaped this person? What were they afraid of? What did they believe they were doing right?* I still write about harm and loss—but I try to do it from a place of understanding, not accusation.

And finally, compassion shapes how I write for readers. I didn't always think about the person on the other side of the page—how they might experience the story, how it might touch or challenge them. For a long time, I was focused on craft—getting the prose just right. But eventually, I realized that someone else would be sitting with my words, bringing their own memories, hopes, and wounds to the reading experience.

Now, compassion reminds me to write in a way that respects the reader and honors their presence. That doesn't mean simplifying or pleasing—it means I want readers to see something they haven't seen before—or to feel seen themselves.

For me, writing with compassion has been transformational. My stories feel more honest. And perhaps most importantly, I'm writing to connect—with others, and with myself. Compassion is not just a personal value—it's a creative principle. And most of all, it helps me stay human. That's what writing is really about.

Compassion as the Writer's Journey

This book is a guide to bringing compassion into every aspect of your creative life.

- **Compassion for Yourself as a Writer**—Writing takes courage. Self-compassion helps you quiet your internal critical voice, accept imperfection, and relax and enjoy the process. I'll share techniques for building confidence, overcoming self-doubt, and writing with honesty.
- **Compassion for Others**—Empathy deepens storytelling. Whether you're writing about real people or fictional characters, I'll explore how to portray them authentically—especially when writing about painful experiences and people who have hurt you.
- **Compassion for Your Readers**—Writing is a way of connecting with others. I'll talk about how to consider your readers and handle sensitive material thoughtfully.
- **Compassion in the Writing Process**—From battling writer's block to facing rejection, I'll offer tools for making your writing practice more sustainable and fulfilling.

The Compassionate Writer

An Invitation to Write with Compassion

Each chapter of this book is designed to help you wherever you are on your writing journey. Inside, you'll find:

- **Clear explanations** of the emotional challenges writers often face—like self-doubt, perfectionism, and fear—and how compassion can help address those feelings. You'll learn how to work through these challenges using psychological insights and practical tools.
- **Exercises** to help you apply each chapter's core ideas. These include freewriting, structured reflection, rewriting from different perspectives, and using a metaphor to explore ideas and emotions.
- **Examples and stories** from my own life as a writer and literary journal editor, along with additional ones from published authors.
- **Writing prompts** to help you explore each chapter's theme through your own voice, guiding you through emotional or creative blocks as you create new material.
- **Guided visualizations** to offer quiet moments for reflection. They help you step out of your busy mind, take an inner journey, and reconnect with your creative purpose—allowing you to return to your writing with renewed clarity and courage. You can use them in whatever way feels most natural: read them silently, record and listen to them with your eyes closed, or simply carry them in your mind and imagine the journey as you go.

Anne E. Beall, PhD

As you move through this book, I hope not only that your writing grows stronger, but that it also deepens your self-understanding and your connection to others. I hope it brings more ease to your process, and more clarity to your stories.

People often ask who I wrote this book for. I wrote it for memoirists—and for writers of character-driven fiction that explores inner lives, emotional landscapes, and human complexity. I wrote it for writers who are hard on themselves, who wrestle with self-doubt, who wonder if they're "real" writers. They may not have an MFA or a publishing deal, but they care deeply about writing well and writing truthfully.

This book is also for writers who've been at it for years—seasoned writers—who may have lost touch with something vital: kindness toward themselves, and curiosity about their work.

So this book is for you. Wherever you are on your path.

Take a breath. Open your notebook or turn on your computer. The story you're here to tell is one only you can write. Welcome to the journey of becoming a compassionate writer.

Let's begin.

Chapter 1: Yes, You Have a Story

"There is no greater agony than bearing an untold story inside you." — Maya Angelou

When I sit down to start a new piece, I can feel the energy flowing out of my fingers. I envision the words flowing onto the page, creating something that will be read widely. But before long, I start thinking: *Who are you kidding? This isn't good. No one is going to read this. Why are you wasting your time?*

Sound familiar? I know I'm not alone. These doubts make it hard to write. But even in those moments when I questioned whether I had something valuable to say, I usually did.

I believe every story has value—whether it's a memoir of your own experiences or a fictional tale from your imagination. And you are worthy of writing your story simply because you exist. You have a perspective no one else does. It's shaped by your life experiences, your dreams, and the things you've learned along the way. That perspective makes your voice one of a kind. Your story is waiting to be told, and only you can tell it. So yes, you have a story.

Why We Doubt Ourselves

In today's world, it's incredibly easy to compare ourselves to hundreds or even thousands of other people online. Social media allows us to see carefully curated versions of others' lives, filtered through a lens that often hides failure or struggle. Everyone around us can seem wildly successful, no matter the field. And writers? They can make it all look effortless—like they just sit down and, voilà, out pops another novel.

It's no wonder we sometimes question whether we're capable of writing that novel, that story, or even that grocery list. There are many reasons we doubt our abilities when it comes to writing. Here are some of the most common:

- **We have unrealistic expectations of writing.** You may believe that writing should come easily. I fall into this trap myself. But the truth is, writing is work. Even the best writers revise, struggle, and spend time getting their ideas into print.
- **We compare ourselves to others.** You might think, *I'll never write as well as that famous author,* or *someone else has already told this story better than I ever could.*
- **We underestimate our own experiences.** You may think your life is too ordinary to write about.
- **We second-guess our imagination.** Maybe you think, *It's silly to write this fictional story in my head. No one will care about it.*
- **We fear vulnerability and rejection.** Whether we're writing about real experiences or inventing a story, it can feel scary to put a part of ourselves into the world. Even if we manage to get it in front of other people, we worry they won't like it, or that the piece will be rejected.
- **We think we need more training.** You might believe that without a Master of Fine Arts (MFA) or a degree in English, you can't write "properly."
- **We assume our story has already been told.** You might think, *Why bother? This has already been done better—in a book or film.*

The Compassionate Writer

Underneath these doubts are some common beliefs—that only extraordinary lives or highly trained people are the ones who should write stories. But that's simply not true. Writing is a skill. It can be learned and developed. I don't believe there is a "writer gene" that predisposes some people to be able to write well. Great stories resonate because they're honest, relatable, and deeply human—not because they're perfect or original.

And when it comes to training, I don't have an MFA, and it never held me back. In fact, most of the writers I know don't have one either. Many didn't even major in English. Elizabeth Gilbert mentions in her book *Big Magic* that no Nobel Prize winners in Literature have MFAs, and four of these laureates only graduated from high school.

It's often said that most stories have already been told—love, loss, betrayal, redemption. And it's true: these themes have echoed through centuries, from ancient myths to Shakespeare and beyond. But *your* story hasn't been told. Not with your voice. Not through your lens. What makes a story matter isn't whether the theme is entirely original—it's the way you shape it. Your insight. Your choices. Your perspective. That's what transforms something timeless into something truly personal and powerful.

You don't need a dramatic life to write something meaningful. We all have stories that matter. Maybe you have a story about someone who helped you in a time of crisis. Or maybe you've gone through a painful breakup and learned something important about yourself. Perhaps you want to capture small, easily overlooked moments—an exchange with your child, a quiet walk in nature, or something in daily life that others don't readily see. Maybe you've written an essay about politics, consumerism, or even toads.

Whatever it is, there's something you care about—and there are readers who want to hear what you have to say.

As the founder and editor of *Chicago Story Press Literary Journal*, I've published countless stories drawn from everyday life—stories that mattered deeply to the writers and to many readers. Most weren't grand or sensational. They were quiet, thoughtful reflections that revealed something important about themselves or about the world.

I've published pieces about relationships slowly unraveling, about what it's like to look at a spouse while aging and reflect on a life built together. I've published stories about helping someone with an addiction, escaping an abusive situation, and coming to terms with regrets that, in hindsight, were never deserved. These stories reveal something that resonates with readers.

If the story you want to tell is fictional, it's just as meaningful. Maybe a character has come to life in your mind, and you want to share this person with others. Maybe you've imagined a world so vivid you want others to experience it. Or maybe you want to write the story you've always longed to read—but haven't found yet.

Give Yourself Permission to Write

The first step is to give yourself permission to write freely—whether your story comes from personal experience or imagination. You don't need anyone's approval to tell your story, and you don't have to justify why it's worth telling.

Your writing doesn't need to be phenomenal from the start. Writing isn't about perfection—it's about discovery. It's about giving yourself the freedom to put thoughts and characters on the

The Compassionate Writer

page and trusting in the process. You can revise later. But first, give yourself permission to begin.

Natalie Goldberg, in her brilliant book *Writing Down the Bones*, encourages writers to keep the pen moving—or fingers typing—and to let whatever wants to come out emerge. Goldberg explains that our first thoughts are often the most powerful because they haven't been edited or filtered by the ego. Sometimes, the prose that spills out in those moments is the most fabulous—precisely because we've stepped out of our own way.

Don't overthink. Just write.

Exercise: Finding the Story Only You Can Tell

Below are some suggestions for finding your story. Take some time to write freely in response to them. Let your thoughts flow without worrying about structure, grammar, or whether your ideas "make sense."

Option 1: Reflect on Your Life

If you want to write about your own life, use these prompts to explore meaningful moments:

- **Turning points:** Write about three moments when a decision, experience, or realization changed your life. Describe each moment in detail: What led up to it? What happened? How did it change you?
- **Small but significant moments:** Think about a brief interaction, a fleeting observation, or an everyday experience. Describe it with sensory detail. What are the reasons this moment has stayed with you? What might it reveal about you or your world?

- **A moment of crisis:** Recall a time when you went through something difficult. Explore what happened, how you reacted, and what you learned from the experience. Looking back, do you see this moment differently now than you did at the time? *Note: please approach difficult memories with care. If it feels overwhelming, give yourself permission to pause, step away, or skip it entirely.*
- **Defining memories:** List three to five of the most vivid memories of your life. Write about each in detail. Then, step back and reflect: What do these moments have in common? What are the reasons they stand out? What do they reveal about your values, fears, desires, or identity?

Option 2: Reflect on Your Imagination

If you feel drawn to writing fiction, use these prompts to explore your creative ideas:

- **The character who speaks to you:** Is there a character you've imagined—a voice or personality that won't leave you alone? Describe them in detail. What do they look like? How do they move, speak, or think? What are some things they have said or done? What story do they want you to tell? Summarize their story in a few sentences.
- **The story you wish existed:** Think about a story you've always wanted to read but haven't found. What is it about? Who are the major characters? Where does it take place? What happens in the story? What makes this story special? Now, imagine you're the one who can bring it to life.

- **The question that intrigues you:** Many great stories start with a compelling question. What idea sparks your curiosity? For example:
    - What if someone woke up with only certain types of memories?
    - What if a distant world existed just beyond our perception?
    - What if someone had a superpower—such as invisibility or superhuman strength—but could only use it in specific situations?

Think of a question that intrigues you and begin imagining a story around it.

Writing Prompts

The following prompts are designed to help you uncover a story *you* can tell. Choose the ones that resonate and simply begin. Don't worry about grammar, structure, or whether it sounds "right." Just let your words flow.

Reclaiming Creative Permission

- Write a page of "bad writing" on purpose—let it be messy, dramatic, silly, or overly sentimental. When you are finished, underline the one sentence that unexpectedly moved you.
- Write a letter to yourself from your future writing self. What encouragement or wisdom do they offer?

Claiming the Value of Your Story

- Imagine that someone steals your life story and turns it into a bestselling book. What kind of book would it be? What are the reasons people would love this story? Describe this book in detail.
- Finish this sentence: "I have a story, and I really should tell it because…" Then keep going. Let the writing lead you wherever it wants to go.

Seeing Your Life as a Story

- Write about a painful experience. What did it teach you about yourself or about life? Tell the true story or reimagine it as fiction.
- Think of someone who taught you something meaningful—but not in the way they intended. Maybe they made a mistake, held an incorrect belief, or simply lived in a way that showed you something important. Write their story and what you learned from it.

Writing from the Imagination: Fiction as Personal Truth

- Create a fictional character who holds a belief about love, worth, fear, or success. What happens when that belief is tested?
- Write about a world where your greatest fear has already come true. What happens?

Reflection Questions (Post-Writing)

Use these after completing any prompt:
- What surprised you while you were writing?

- Did you notice any resistance or fear? Where did it come from?
- What underlies that fear or resistance?
- How did it feel to give yourself permission to write without judgment?

What is a Guided Visualization? How Can It Help Your Writing?

A guided visualization is an imaginative meditation that invites you to step into a vivid, sensory-rich scene in your mind. It's a tool designed to soothe the nervous system, quiet self-judgment, and tap into deeper layers of memory and creativity. Instead of forcing your way into a story, you allow it to surface naturally—through images, feelings, and intuitive impressions.

Here are a few ways to use this one: You can read it slowly, allowing yourself to sink into the imagery. Or, you can record it and listen later with your eyes closed. If you already have a meditation or visualization practice, you can adapt these ideas and weave them into that routine.

Guided Visualization: Ocean of Stories

One way to let your stories come to the surface is to relax and simply allow them to emerge. They're already within you and may need some quiet moments to reveal themselves. What follows is a guided visualization designed to help you let your stories emerge.

Take a moment to sit comfortably, allowing your body to sink into the surface beneath you. Take a deep breath, letting your lungs fill completely, and then slowly exhale. Take another deep breath, and as you release it, feel your shoulders drop and any tension you're carrying just melt away.

Take a few more deep breaths. Inhale gently through your nose, hold it for a moment, and then release it slowly. With each breath, feel yourself becoming more relaxed and your mind becoming quieter.

Now, imagine you're by the ocean. You're standing on a beach with salmon-colored sand stretching endlessly in both directions. Gentle waves roll in, lapping at the shore with a soft, rhythmic sound. A light breeze brushes against your skin—it's just the right mix of warmth and coolness. It's early morning, and you're completely alone on this beautiful beach. You pause to enjoy the soothing sound of the waves, then glance up to see the sun rising slowly in the distance, its face just peeking out where the sky and water meet at the horizon.

You begin walking, noticing how the sand varies—sometimes it shifts slightly under your feet, and at other times it's firmer as you walk closer to the shore. You watch the waves come and go. No two are the same—there's a rhythm here, but it isn't predictable. Some waves almost reach you, while others seem shy and stay farther away.

As each wave rolls in, the color of the ocean shifts—a light green-blue deepens into a rich navy, while the tips of the waves froth into a creamy white.

You pause for a moment, marveling at the enormity of the ocean, then look down at the sand. Scattered along the shore are shells of many shapes and sizes. Some are bleached white from the sun, whereas others look as though they arrived here recently. A few are broken while others are perfectly intact. All of them have been carried here by the water.

The Compassionate Writer

You consider how shells are like stories. They come from the depths of the ocean—sometimes polished, sometimes fragmented—and arrive at the shore to be seen, held, and remembered. Some are visible while others are buried just beneath the surface, but they are present. Over time, they become part of the sand, no longer distinct, but an essential part of the beach.

You reflect on your life and the stories that live within you. Like the ocean, you hold countless moments and ideas, waiting to be brought forth. Some of them are from poignant moments of your life while others are people, worlds, and events you have imagined.

A story begins to rise within you now. Maybe it's a memory—a moment of kindness, a challenge you overcame, or a lesson you learned. Maybe it's a small interaction or a conversation that has stayed with you. Or perhaps it's something you have imagined—a character who's been waiting to come forward or a world you want to share with others.

Consider these thoughts and the stories they could become.

Spend some time thinking about them and how they seem to keep surfacing in your mind. Recall as much as you can. As you think about this, you wonder: Is this a story? Is it a story worth telling?

You continue walking. Up ahead, you see words written in the sand.

"Every story matters. Including yours."

You take a deep breath and know that this is true. Your story matters. You reflect on the story within you. Maybe you don't yet know where it begins or how it will end, but you can feel it. You know there is a story that is waiting to emerge. You only need to give it space, let it arise, and take the time to nurture it and write it.

Take a deep breath.

Trust yourself.

And begin.

Picture the first lines beginning to take shape. Maybe it's an image, a feeling, or a piece of dialogue. You see yourself writing—sitting at your computer or writing with pen and paper—capturing what's inside you.

Stay in this moment for just a little longer. See yourself writing.

When you're ready, gently return to the present moment, carrying with you the inspiration and confidence to take the next step in your writing journey.

*

In the next chapter, I'll explore the common challenge of the inner critic and how self-compassion can help you move through it. But for now, take a small step forward—whether it's jotting down a memory, imagining a character, or brainstorming ideas.

Your story matters, and the world is waiting to hear it.

Chapter 2: The Inner Critic

"If your compassion does not include yourself, it is incomplete." — Jack Kornfield

I am undoubtedly my harshest judge. Like many writers, I'm deeply critical of my own work. I question everything: the quality of my prose, the originality of my ideas, the depth of my reflections, even the length of my published pieces. If criticizing my writing were an Olympic sport, I'd be a strong contender for the gold.

Sometimes, I feel like a fraud—even after publishing books, essays, and short stories.

Apparently, I'm not alone. Almost every writer I know wrestles with self-doubt. Even wildly successful writers have admitted to the same nagging insecurity. Maya Angelou once said, "I have written eleven books, but each time I think, 'Uh oh, they're going to find out now. I've run a game on everybody, and they're going to find me out.'"

That voice that tells us we're not good enough is painfully familiar. And the irony is that although it often claims to be trying to help, it can shut us down right in the middle of the creative process. But if someone like Maya Angelou could hear that voice and still keep writing, it tells us something essential: we don't have to eliminate self-doubt to create meaningful work.

In the rest of this chapter, I'll explore how compassion can help you make peace with that critical voice—and how to use it when it has something helpful to offer.

But first, where does that voice come from?

Anne E. Beall, PhD

Why We're So Hard on Ourselves

According to Tara Mohr, the inner critic reflects our safety instinct—the part of us that wants to avoid emotional risks like rejection, criticism, or failure. But it's cunning. Instead of warning us directly about risk, it takes a more convincing route: it tells us we're not good enough. On some level, this voice is trying to protect us from embarrassment and prevent us from failing.

One reason this voice feels so persuasive is because of the brain's *negativity bias*—our tendency to focus more on what's wrong than what's right. Psychologist Roy Baumeister and his colleagues found that negative experiences, thoughts, and feedback have a significantly stronger impact on us than positive ones. This bias likely helped our ancestors survive by keeping them alert to potential threats—but in creative work, it often causes us to magnify flaws and overlook strengths. That critical voice amplifies fear and self-doubt in an effort to keep us safe.

As a result, the inner critic can hold us back. It might discourage risk-taking, stifle creativity, and keep us from exploring new ideas. The inner critic may whisper things like:

"This is terrible. Other writers are so much better than you."

"You should be further along by now."

"This doesn't seem to come easily to you; maybe you should do something else."

These thoughts can be demoralizing, leading to writer's block, procrastination, or even abandoning a writing project altogether. The real problem is that the inner critic may be delivering vague, unproductive judgments that don't help you improve the work.

The Compassionate Writer

How Self-Compassion Shifts Your Relationship with Writing

Self-compassion helps you manage the inner critic by offering perspective. Struggling with your writing doesn't make you a bad writer—it makes you human. Instead of harshly criticizing yourself, self-compassion invites you to gently acknowledge your frustration and accept that writing can be difficult.

This shift—from judgment to kindness—reduces anxiety and creates space for resilience. In her book *Self-Compassion: The Proven Power of Being Kind to Yourself*, psychologist Kristin Neff explains how self-compassion lowers stress, making it easier to face challenges and keep going when things feel hard.

It also changes the way we think about writing itself. Psychologist Carol Dweck, in *Mindset: The New Psychology of Success*, shows how a fixed mindset tells us, *If this doesn't come easily, I must not be good at it.* In contrast, a growth mindset says, *If this is hard, it's because I'm learning.* The struggle becomes part of the process—not a sign to stop, but a reason to continue.

Writing, like anything else, improves with practice. You probably didn't master riding a bike or dancing from an instruction manual. Most of us learn by doing—and writing is no different. The more you write, the more you grow. That doesn't mean ignoring the areas that need work. It means approaching them with curiosity instead of harsh self-criticism. When you meet your work with patience and self-kindness, you create space for real growth.

And guess what? Even the most celebrated writers have wrestled with doubt. John Steinbeck wrote in his journal, "I'm not a writer. I've been fooling myself and other people"—*while* working on *The Grapes of Wrath*, after *Of Mice and Men* had already made him famous. The voice of doubt never really disappears. But it doesn't have to stop us.

Much of what the inner critic says is fueled by perfectionism—the habit of comparing our work to impossible standards. As Anne Lamott reminds us, "Perfectionism is the voice of the oppressor, the enemy of the people." It's one of the inner critic's favorite disguises, demanding flawlessness and paralyzing us in the process. But as Lamott explains, good writing doesn't come from chasing perfection; it comes from giving ourselves permission to write badly, especially at the beginning.

When the Inner Critic is Helpful

The trick with the inner critic is knowing when to engage with it—and how to use it in ways that offer real value. That means learning to manage when and how it shows up in your process. A well-managed inner critic can:

- Push you to improve—It may point out areas in your writing that need more clarity, depth, or revision.
- Encourage discipline—It can remind you to keep working, revising, and striving to grow.
- Act as a filter—It can help you recognize when an idea needs more development.

The problem isn't that we have an inner critic—the issue is that this voice can take over and squash creativity rather than encouraging growth. The goal isn't to silence it completely, but to retrain it to work for you rather than against you.

The Compassionate Writer

Practical Steps to Manage the Inner Critic

Acknowledge Your Inner Critic

The first step to quieting the inner critic is simply noticing when it shows up. As you write, pay attention to your thoughts. Are you being hard on yourself? Are you feeling frustrated or unkind toward your work? Don't judge yourself for having these thoughts—just notice them. Take a deep breath and let the thoughts pass, as much as you can. Sometimes, simply recognizing that the inner critic is speaking can help diminish its power.

Respond to Your Inner Critic

When you notice the inner critic getting loud or insistent, pause and take a breath. Offer yourself words of encouragement to counter these thoughts. For example, if your inner critic says you'll never finish your piece, you could respond: "It's okay to feel overwhelmed. Every writer feels like this sometimes. I'm going to keep taking it one step at a time."

Embrace Imperfection

Writing doesn't have to be perfect—especially not in the early stages. The first draft is a place to discover and explore your thoughts. It's meant to be messy. When you allow yourself to write imperfectly, you free yourself to consider new ideas and find your voice.

When you let go of perfection, writing can become joyful—you might stumble across old memories, uncover new ways of thinking, notice hidden patterns, or meet characters who feel like old friends. Sometimes, when I manage to quiet my inner critic, I'm astonished by what flows onto the page, reading my own words and wondering,

Who wrote that? It's as if the words came through me, not from me—and that's the beauty of letting go.

Engaging the Inner Critic at Different Points in the Process

The inner critic can be a real pain at some stages of writing, but surprisingly helpful during others. The key is to engage with it when it serves your writing, not when it shuts you down.

When you're drafting, I recommend ignoring your inner critic entirely. Tell them to go away—better yet, hand them a one-way ticket to the Bahamas. Remind them to enjoy the sunshine, sip a piña colada, and stay far away from your writing space. Then, just write. Let the words flow. Let it be messy. This is the stage for exploration, not evaluation.

Later, once you've had some distance from your draft, you can gently invite the critic back in—but on your terms. Ask for helpful feedback: What could make this piece stronger? What's missing? Don't accept comments that belittle you. You're not asking whether you're a real writer—you're asking how the writing can be improved. That distinction matters.

As you move toward the final stages, it's okay to let your inner critic become a bit more critical. This is the time to look closely at structure, clarity, and detail. Encourage them to tell you everything they can—but remind them who's boss. Let them do their work—but don't forget they work for you, not the other way around.

Keep in mind that you get to choose when and how to engage your inner critic. It doesn't run the show. You do.

The Compassionate Writer

Build a Set of Compassionate Responses

At the end of this chapter, there is an exercise where you have a dialogue with your inner critic, explore their motivations, and give compassionate responses. Once you've completed this exercise, you will have a powerful tool at your disposal—a set of ready-made replies for moments when you experience self-doubt.

The next time that critical voice speaks up, respond with one of the responses you've written. With practice, this will become second nature, helping you replace negativity with understanding and encouragement.

Over time, you'll train yourself to engage with your inner critic in a healthier, more constructive way—one that supports your growth as a writer rather than holding you back. Remember, the goal isn't to silence your inner critic completely, but to reshape its voice into one that motivates, guides, and strengthens you.

The Transformative Power of Managing Your Inner Critic

By managing your inner critic, you set yourself on the path to writing—and to enjoying the process.

Our internal voices aren't always right or helpful. I've written pieces I initially thought were brilliant, only to revisit them later and realize they needed far more work than I'd imagined. Other times, I've struggled to get even a few paragraphs on the page, convinced by my inner critic that I had no idea what I was doing—only to return later and find something valuable.

Writing takes time, and it's rarely effortless. Some days, the words will flow easily. Other days, they won't. Either way, it's okay. What matters is showing up, trusting the process, and allowing yourself the space to grow.

Learning to manage your inner critic is ultimately a gift of compassion and a way of coming to trust yourself. It means learning to separate the criticisms that help from the ones that don't. It means realizing that one off day—or one rough draft—doesn't define you as a writer. It also means giving yourself permission to write imperfectly, to revise, and to keep going. You begin to understand that the process matters more than any single moment of success or struggle.

And perhaps most powerfully, when you learn how to engage your inner critic, you begin to transform that voice—not just in your writing, but in other areas of your life as well.

Exercise: A Conversation with Your Inner Critic

One way of interacting with your inner critic is to engage with it on the page. By writing out a conversation, you can explore its true motives and determine how you want to respond.

Step 1: Meet Your Inner Critic

Before starting the dialogue, take a moment to picture your inner critic. Ask yourself:

- What's their name? (Some possibilities: Ed, The Judge, Miss Perfect, The Ghost of My High School English Teacher.)
- What do they look like? Maybe they're a stiff, formal professor, or a nervous wreck wringing their hands. Perhaps they're a drill sergeant barking orders. Picture them in your mind.

Step 2: Write a Dialogue and Uncover Your Inner Critic's Motives

Let your inner critic speak first. What do they say when you sit down to write? Start by giving them the floor—let them launch into one of their familiar monologues. What doubts or judgments do they throw your way? Don't hold back—let them say it all.

Describe their body language, their tone of voice, their facial expressions. Are they sharp-eyed and sneering? Tired and exasperated? Maybe they pace the room or lean in close with crossed arms. Make them real.

Then, challenge them and ask some questions such as:

- "Why are you criticizing me?"
- "Are you trying to help me or hurt me?"
- "What are the reasons you say that?"
- "If I always listened to you, what do you think would happen?"
- "If I ignored you completely, what would be likely to occur?"

Some inner critics are trying to protect us from failure, whereas others are just echoes of past doubts and negativity. By questioning the inner critic, you can understand their true motives.

Step 3: Responding to Your Inner Critic and Redefining their Role

Now that you understand your inner critic's motivations, it's time to shift the conversation. Instead of letting their words hold you back, respond with self-compassion. Review what your inner critic said in your dialogue from Step Two. Then, write a response that acknowledges their concerns but also supports your creativity rather than stifling it. Here is an example.

Inner Critic: "You'll never be able to write as well as that famous writer."

Response: "I don't need to write like anyone else. My unique voice is special, and no one else can tell the story I'm here to tell."

Inner Critic: "I read what you've written, and it's terrible."

Response: "First drafts—sometimes even second and third drafts—aren't always great. Writing is a process of refining drafts over time."

Inner Critic: "You don't have the training or skill to do this well."

Response: "Writing is a lifelong learning process. No one knows everything at the start, and it's okay to seek help, take classes, or read books to improve. I'm already growing just by writing."

If you sense that your inner critic is trying to help, consider giving them a new role—one that supports you. Continue your dialogue and ask if they can assist in a more constructive way. Maybe they can hold their critiques until you're ready for revisions, stepping in as an editor when the time is right. Or perhaps they can shift from being a harsh judge to a coach who offers encouragement and guidance. Instead of letting your inner critic be a bully, invite them to be a mentor—one who helps you grow rather than shutting you down.

The Compassionate Writer

Writing Prompts

These prompts are designed to help you see your inner critic from a new perspective, spark your creativity, and get you writing. Use them to explore your thoughts and transform your inner critic into a more constructive voice.

Exploring Your Inner Critic in New Ways

- Your inner critic might remind you of someone from your life. Who is it? What traits of theirs show up in your critic's voice—and which ones don't? Explore what aspects of this person are incorporated and which ones are not.
- Your inner critic was once a brilliant writer—until something happened that left them bitter and harsh. What was their downfall? Write their backstory and tell us about what happened to them.

Why You're Hard on Yourself

- What did you learn about achievement, perfection, or failure when you were growing up? Write a scene from childhood or adolescence that may have helped shape the voice of your inner critic.
- What are the standards you hold for yourself? How realistic are these standards? Describe them and which ones are reasonable and which ones are not.

Playing with Perspective

- Rewrite a story where your inner critic is the hero. What do they say and do that makes them the hero?

Interacting with the Inner Critic

- Imagine you are conducting a performance review for your inner critic. What feedback do you give them? What are they doing well? Where have they made mistakes? Be specific—and honest in your appraisal.

Embracing Imperfection

- Take a moment to create something that is flawed—don't worry about punctuation, full-length sentences, or even making any kind of sense. Imagine you are writing only for yourself. Take a half-baked idea and just start writing it out or draft some dialogue that you know isn't great. Just write without stopping. Then put away your draft, and review it after a couple of days have passed. Do you see anything of value? What did you learn from this experience?

When Self-Doubt is Useful

- Describe a time when self-doubt helped you improve your work. What did you change because of it?

The Compassionate Writer

Guided Visualization: Meet Your Inner Critic

Earlier, you met your inner critic through structured writing. Now, you'll connect with that voice through a guided visualization that leans into intuition and emotion. Some writers find this approach reveals hidden feelings or unexpected insights that structured exercises can't always provide.

In this guided visualization, you will meet your inner critic and have a conversation. Take a deep breath in, filling your lungs completely, and then slowly exhale. With each breath, let your body relax a little more. Feel your shoulders drop, your face soften, and your jaw release.

There is nothing to do. Nowhere else to be. Just take the time to breathe and sink into this moment. Take several deep breaths and then exhale them slowly.

Now, imagine walking down a long, quiet hallway where your footsteps echo against the floor. Along the corridor are doors, each one labeled with a different aspect of you—Doubt, Creativity, Memories, Dreams. As you walk past, you can almost sense what lies behind each one.

As you move forward, you notice a door at the very end on the left. A bold sign on it reads: *Inner Critic*.

Something inside you hesitates. You take a deep breath. Then, with curiosity, you reach for the handle and open the door.

The room is cluttered, as if someone has been working tirelessly for years without ever pausing to tidy up. Two large windows along one wall are grimy, and you can't even see out of them. Stacks of books rest on desks and chairs, some open to pages filled with notes, others covered in dust. Papers are scattered across the floor with red ink scrawled across them. Crossed-out sentences, circled words, harsh critiques such as "not good enough" and "start over" are scribbled in the margins.

One wall is covered in whiteboards, filled with endless corrections, question marks, and frantic notes. The air feels thick with negative thoughts and abandoned ideas.

Your Inner Critic is in the center of this room.

Who are they?

What do they look like?

Maybe they are a younger version of you. Or perhaps they are a strict teacher, an exasperated editor, or a disapproving parent. Take a moment to see them clearly in your mind.

Notice their expression. Are they overwhelmed or unhappy or irritated?

"Hello," you say.

Your Inner Critic looks up, studying you. For a moment, they don't respond. Then, with a small gesture, they invite you to step further inside.

As you move into the room, you take a deep breath and ask, "Why do you criticize me so much?"

Your Inner Critic hesitates. Something flickers across their face. Then, finally, they speak.

Listen to what they say about why they criticize you. Take it in, without judgment. Let the words settle.

Now, consider how you want to respond.

Do you want to challenge them? To ask more questions? To remind them that perfection isn't the goal?

Tell them what you believe—and what you want them to understand.

As you speak, notice how the feeling in the room changes.

The Compassionate Writer

Your Inner Critic listens. Maybe they argue. Maybe they hesitate. Maybe they shift as they consider your words.

Let the conversation unfold. Tell them exactly what you need them to do. Be explicit.

When you're ready, move toward the door. If there's anything else you need to say, feel free to say it now. If they have anything else to tell you, just listen.

When you're ready, step back into the hallway, closing the door behind you. Take a deep breath in, feeling clear and peaceful. Exhale slowly.

Your Inner Critic still exists, but they no longer control you. You can return to this room anytime—to listen, to understand, and to remind them (and yourself) of the role you want them to play in your writing.

Now, return to the present moment, carrying this sense of freedom with you. Write something. Let the words flow.

*

In the next chapter, I'll explore how to embrace vulnerability in your writing and how it can help deepen your work.

Chapter 3: Self-Compassion and Embracing Vulnerability

"Vulnerability is not winning or losing; it's having the courage to show up and be seen when we have no control over the outcome. Vulnerability is not weakness; it's our greatest measure of courage."
— Brené Brown

Writing authentically—whether in memoir or fiction—requires vulnerability. To create stories and characters that feel real, you have to look closely at your own life, confront the uncomfortable parts, and bring them to the page. That willingness to face what's difficult, instead of turning away, is what makes writing an act of courage.

But that kind of honesty often means making peace with your fears, regrets, and failures. It requires looking at your past self—your choices, your pain, your patterns—with empathy instead of judgment. Vulnerability asks you to open the door. Self-compassion is what keeps you from slamming it shut when something painful walks in.

It also means seeing both the positive and negative aspects of yourself—and meeting them with acceptance. That includes acknowledging the parts you don't like and admitting they belong to you. These might be qualities others have pointed out over the years—the ones we prefer to explain away as circumstances or someone else's fault. Deep down, though, we know they're ours.

In my case, I can be blunt and overly critical. I'm sometimes judgmental and impatient, and I don't like admitting that—but it's true. I also know I have many wonderful qualities: I'm generous, kind, and quick to help when someone needs it. Because I can look

The Compassionate Writer

at myself with compassion, I'm able to hold both the good and the difficult parts of my personality. And that kind of honest self-awareness helps me see my past—and the people in my life—with compassion, too.

That's a hallmark of some of the writing that stays with us. Think of the books or essays that have lingered in your mind. They weren't written by someone playing it safe—they came from someone willing to show the messy, complicated truth about themselves and about life. Maybe it was a memoir where the writer shared something she was ashamed of, or a novel where the protagonist was deeply flawed. These works resonate because they reveal something real about being human.

Some of the most widely read pieces I've published in *Chicago Story Press Literary Journal* are the ones that tackle life's most difficult moments. Writers have shared experiences of wanting to end their lives, of being victimized by those in power, or of navigating intimacy after surviving breast cancer. These authors didn't shy away from the hardest moments—they embraced them. Through their writing, they invited readers into the reality of their vulnerability, showing what it feels like to be exposed, uncertain, and profoundly human.

But being vulnerable isn't easy. Like many writers, I've found it difficult to make myself truly open—to reveal the embarrassing parts of my life story to others. It's much easier to write about other people's mistakes than to expose my own. Yet when I've been honest about my flaws and my history, I've produced some of my best work—the pieces that resonate most with readers. I've written about my estrangement from family members and my complicated relationship with my mother.

Vulnerability alone, though, is not enough. Simply sharing experiences you're ashamed of, or that feel deeply personal, isn't what makes writing powerful—it's the meaning you draw from them, which I'll discuss in the next chapter. The first step, however, is embracing vulnerability. When you do, you invite readers into your world and create a powerful bridge between you and your audience.

Finding Your Voice Through the Story Only You Can Tell

Once you begin to approach your experiences with compassion and honesty, you also begin to discover something deeper—your unique voice as a writer.

But what exactly is voice? In writing, voice is the unique personality that comes through on the page—the combination of tone, word choice, rhythm, and perspective that makes a piece of writing unmistakably yours. It's not just what you say, but how you say it. Just as you can recognize a friend's voice in a crowded room, readers can recognize a writer's voice across different stories.

Here are three examples of distinct voices:

- **Wry and Observant**: "Everyone at the table was pretending to enjoy the casserole, except Aunt Marlene, who had long since given up lying about food." This voice uses humor and dry understatement to reveal character and mood.
- **Lyrical and Reflective**: "The wind moved through the wheat fields like breath through a sleeping house, slow and steady and full of secrets." This voice leans into poetic imagery, evoking emotion through metaphor and rhythm.

- **Direct and Vulnerable**: "I didn't expect to cry when I saw the house again. I thought I'd moved on. But there it was, same porch light, same ache."

This voice feels raw and emotionally honest, letting simple sentences convey the weight of feeling.

Each of these voices tells us something about the narrator's personality, values, and emotions. The key is that voice is not something you force—it's something you uncover by writing honestly and by leaning into the language that feels most natural to you.

Tone is part of voice, too. If voice is the personality behind the words, tone is the emotional filter—playful, tender, wry, fierce, formal, conversational. It's the feeling that washes over the reader as they move through your prose. The same story can land completely differently depending on the tone you choose. A dry, understated tone might make readers laugh; a raw, vulnerable tone might make them cry.

Voice emerges when emotional honesty meets the natural rhythms of your language. That combination is what makes your writing unmistakably yours.

And you can tell when an author's voice is genuine. Their words feel intimate, as if they're speaking just to you. Even if you've never met them, their voice is recognizable—distinct as a fingerprint.

For me, I know I've found my voice when I stop trying to impress or explain and simply tell the truth. That's when the writing feels most alive and most like "me." And that often requires vulnerability and honesty.

Finding your voice means finding your story—and that often involves stepping into parts of yourself you'd rather avoid. One of the clearest explanations of this comes from Anne Lamott in her book *Bird by Bird*:

> "We write to expose the unexposed. If there is one door in the castle you have been told not to go through, you must. Otherwise, you'll be rearranging furniture in rooms you've already been. Most human beings are dedicated to keeping that one door shut. But the writer's job is to see what's behind it, to see the bleak unspeakable stuff, and to turn the unspeakable into words—not just any words but if we can, into rhythm and blues.
>
> You can't do this without discovering your own true voice, and you can't find your true voice and peer behind the door and report honestly and clearly to us if your parents are reading over your shoulder. They are probably the ones who told you not to open that door in the first place."

How Vulnerability Creates Emotional Truth on the Page

In both memoir and fiction, readers can sense when a writer is being emotionally honest—and when they're holding back. When we allow ourselves to be vulnerable, we share the deeper truths that readers are often wondering about. We write from a place of authenticity, where characters feel real and conflicts carry genuine emotional weight. As a result, the work resonates more deeply—because readers recognize something of themselves in it.

Here are two examples of the same event. In the first one, the writer is not embracing their vulnerability—they seem to be holding back. And in the second example, they are more emotionally honest.

Holding back: I visited my father in the hospital last week. He looked tired as he reached for my hand. We spoke for a few minutes about the weather and the forecast for the next few days. I stayed for an hour, then went home.

Emotionally honest: I visited my father in the hospital last week. His skin was tinged with grey, and when he reached for my hand, his fingers felt thin, fragile, and unfamiliar. We talked about the weather, as if discussing regular things could keep us safe from the truth sitting between us. I stayed for an hour, pretending I wasn't counting the seconds, then went home, gripping the steering wheel like it might keep me from falling apart.

The Barriers to Vulnerability

Being vulnerable isn't easy. For many of us, the barrier isn't just self-doubt—it's the memory of real consequences. Maybe you once confided in a friend or shared something deeply personal with someone you loved—and it didn't go the way you hoped. Experiences like these leave a mark and teach us that opening up can lead to pain. There are many reasons it can be hard to be vulnerable with others. Here are some of the most common barriers.

Fear of Judgment

Accessing our vulnerability can be deeply challenging, and one of the biggest reasons we hold back is fear of judgment. Sometimes, it's the inner critic warning us not to say too much. It whispers that certain details are too personal, too messy, too risky to share: *This is too much. You're going to regret putting that out there. What will people think of you when they read this?*

Whether we're writing about our own lives or creating fictional characters, it can feel terrifying to imagine how others might react.

Will they see me differently? Will they judge me? That fear of being misunderstood, rejected, or exposed can stop us before we even begin.

Self-compassion can help you to address this fear. By accepting your imperfections, you can release that pressure to be universally liked. What matters is that you're telling your story with honesty and heart. Allowing yourself to be vulnerable means trusting that the people who need to connect with your words will do so—and that the ones who judge you are reflecting their own fears, not yours.

Shame

Shame is another major barrier to vulnerability. When we write about our most difficult experiences, we may be ashamed of what we've been through, about the mistakes we've made, or about the emotions we've experienced. Shame tells us to stay silent and to hide the parts of ourselves we think are unworthy of being seen.

Roxane Gay's *Hunger* is a powerful memoir about body image, trauma, and shame. She revealed that as difficult as it was to write about being sexually assaulted, she felt compelled to do so. "Something terrible happened. That something terrible broke me. I wish I could leave it at that, but this is a memoir of my body, so I need to tell you what happened to my body." She goes on to share one of the most intimate and painful truths of her life—she was gang-raped at the age of twelve.

Gay's memoir also explores how she coped with trauma, revealing that her eating disorder became a way to bury her pain. She wrote, "I was swallowing my secrets and making my body expand and explode. I found ways to hide in plain sight, to keep feeding a hunger that could never be satisfied—the hunger to stop hurting." In seeing protection within her body, she ultimately found herself trapped within it.

These are painful truths to share. And yet Gay's honesty has helped many readers reflect on their own relationships with their bodies and the ways we use food—or other forms of coping—to manage emotional wounds.

Writing *Hunger* was immensely difficult; Gay has said it was the hardest project she ever undertook. Although she often felt ashamed of her past and the choices she made, telling her story showed others they're not alone in their pain. For the millions of Americans who have experienced an eating disorder or sexual assault, this is a story that matters. By writing openly about her experiences, Gay challenged the idea that trauma and shame must be hidden. In doing so, she found catharsis—but also created dialogue and a space for collective healing. Her work reminds us that vulnerability isn't weakness—it's essential for healing.

Self-compassion helps us approach shame with gentleness and clarity. Writing through it, instead of avoiding it, can be freeing. It allows you to reclaim your story and stop letting shame decide how (or if) it gets told.

Legal and Ethical Issues

I talk about these issues in more detail in Chapter Five, but here's the short version: One of the biggest barriers to vulnerability is the fear of getting into legal trouble. When you write about real people—especially in nonfiction, memoir, or personal essays—you may wonder, *Can I even say this? What if they get angry? What if they sue me?*

Legally, defamation means making a false statement, presenting it as fact, and causing harm to someone's reputation. Written defamation is *libel*. For someone to win a case, they usually have to prove the statement was false, presented as fact (not opinion), shared with others, and that it caused harm. If they're a public figure, it has to have been said with "actual malice" (you knew it was false or didn't check). Still, even baseless claims can be stressful and costly to navigate, so it's wise to understand your rights before you publish. If you're unsure, consult a legal professional who can help you assess the risks and clarify the laws that apply to your work.

Ethically, the questions get trickier. Even if you *can* legally write something, should you? Will telling this story cause unnecessary harm to someone's privacy or dignity? Will it reveal things that aren't yours to share? Writing with vulnerability doesn't mean disregarding the impact your words may have on others. Sometimes the ethical choice is to change names, alter details, or ask permission—while still telling the emotional truth of your story.

Embracing Vulnerability in Memoir Writing

In memoir, vulnerability is essential. But it's not just about recounting painful events—it's about revealing how those moments felt. Readers don't want just the facts; they're looking for the emotions behind them. What was it like to grow up in a difficult family? How did it feel to lose someone you loved or face a personal crisis? What mistakes did you make, and how did they shape you? The more honestly you explore these questions, the more deeply readers will connect with your story.

In *How to Slowly Kill Yourself and Others in America*, Kiese Laymon writes:

> "I lie in a bathtub of cold water, still sweating and singing love songs to myself. I put the gun to my head and cock it. I think of my Grandma and remember that old feeling of being so in love that nothing matters except seeing and being seen by her. I drop the gun to my chest. I'm so sad, and I can't really see a way out of what I'm feeling, but I'm leaning on memory for help. Faster. Slower. I think I want to hurt myself more than I'm already hurting. I'm not the smartest boy in the world by a long shot, but even in my funk I know that easy remedies—like eating your way out of sad, or fucking your way out of sad, or lying your way out of sad, or slanging your way out of sad, or robbing your way out of sad, or gambling your way out of sad, or shooting your way out of sad—are just slower, more acceptable ways for desperate folks, and especially paroled Black boys in our country, to kill ourselves and others close to us in America."

Laymon doesn't just tell us what he's thinking and feeling—he immerses us in his unfiltered reality. He is brutally honest about his suicidal thoughts and the memories that pull him back, as well as his realization that his past coping mechanisms won't help him escape his pain.

Readers connect with this kind of vulnerable storytelling because life is messy. When writers are honest about their struggles and mistakes, readers are more likely to see themselves reflected in the story.

Anne E. Beall, PhD

A Self-Compassionate Approach to Memoir Writing

Self-compassion helps you embrace vulnerability. It allows you to face difficult truths with gentleness and understanding—and to remember that you, too, are human. You've lived through painful moments. You've made mistakes. You've failed. Like everyone else, you're imperfect—and that's what makes your story worth telling. Below are some steps to help you be more compassionate as you begin to share those vulnerable moments.

Acknowledge Your Fears

It's natural to feel nervous or afraid when writing about deeply personal experiences. Instead of pushing those feelings away, acknowledge them. If it helps, write about your fears before diving into the story itself. Accepting your emotions allows you to move through them rather than to be paralyzed by them.

Give Yourself Permission to Take Your Time

Writing about personal pain or trauma can be intensely emotional. Sometimes it takes months—or even years—to process an experience before you're ready to put it into words. Take your time. If you feel yourself resisting, trust that instinct; it may simply mean it's not time to begin writing about it.

When you begin, pay attention to how you feel as you write. If the emotions become overwhelming, respect that. Give yourself permission to pause—whether that means taking a short walk, stepping away for a few hours, or even taking a longer break from your manuscript. And if it feels like too much to hold alone, consider talking with a counseling professional to help you process what's coming up. Stepping back doesn't mean you're avoiding the work;

it means you're protecting your well-being so you can return to the page with greater clarity and strength.

Write Without Judgment

In the drafting stage, focus on getting the truth of your story onto the page without worrying about how it will be received. This is your space to be honest with yourself. The time for editing and refining will come later. For now, just write freely. Imagine you're writing this only for yourself. There is no audience.

If your inner critic shows up uninvited, you already have the tools to respond—use the strategies you developed in the previous chapter. Then take a breath and keep writing.

Write in Third-Person POV

Another way to get your story onto the page is to create some distance by writing it in third-person point of view. Instead of telling the story as if it happened to you, try putting it on the page as if it happened to someone else. That distance can make it easier to write honestly, without feeling overwhelmed.

For example, maybe someone hurt you deeply, and it's hard to face that pain on the page. Try creating a character based on yourself. Give them a different name. Tell the story through their eyes—what happened, how it felt, and what shifted before, during, and after. By changing the lens, you may find you can say things that felt too vulnerable when it was "you" on the page.

Revisit the Past with Compassion

Most importantly, once your story is on the page, take a step back and try to understand it. Look gently at the version of yourself who lived through those moments. What were you going through at the time? What fears, pressures, or beliefs shaped your choices? What resources did you have—or not have? Instead of asking, *Why did I do that?*, try asking *What did I need?*

Memoir isn't just about what happened—it's about what it meant. And that meaning emerges when we stop seeing ourselves only as we are now, and start viewing our past selves with curiosity and kindness. The goal isn't to justify or condemn—it's to understand.

Self-compassion means allowing yourself to be seen fully—not just in fragments of shame or righteousness, but in all your complexity.

As you reflect, ask yourself:

- What did I believe at the time?
- What was I afraid of?
- What was I trying to protect or achieve—even if imperfectly?
- What part of me was just trying to survive?
- What didn't I know yet?

Revisiting your story through these questions allows you to move from judgment to understanding. You don't have to make yourself look good. You only have to tell the emotional truth.

When you write about yourself with compassion, you deepen your storytelling. You reveal complexity, contradiction, and transformation. And in doing so, you invite your reader to see not only who you were—but who they might be, too.

Embracing Vulnerability in Fiction Writing

Although fiction might seem like a safer space to avoid vulnerability because you're writing about imagined characters, it is still important. Readers crave characters who feel real. Creating those characters requires tapping into your own life and exploring your vulnerabilities.

In fiction, vulnerability often emerges through how you write about fear, failure, longing, and loss. It's about crafting characters who are flawed, who make mistakes, and who struggle with difficult emotions. Creating characters who feel fully human will often require you to draw from your own emotional experiences. You want your readers to feel what you've felt—even if it's uncomfortable.

A powerful example of vulnerability in fiction comes from Toni Morrison's *Beloved*, a novel that explores grief, trauma, and love. Many of the characters are profoundly vulnerable, haunted by the brutalities that occurred while they were enslaved. Sethe, a central female character, commits an unthinkable act—she kills her own daughter to prevent the girl from being returned to slavery at Sweet Home, the plantation where Sethe endured horrific abuse. When Paul D learns what she has done, he confronts her. Their exchange reveals the depth of Sethe's pain and conviction:

> "It worked," she said.
> "How? Your boys gone—you don't know where. One girl dead, the other won't leave the yard. How did it work?"

> "They ain't at Sweet Home. Schoolteacher ain't got 'em."
>
> "Maybe there's worse."
>
> "It ain't my job to know what's worse. It's my job to know what is and to keep them away from what I know is terrible. I did that."

This moment captures the ultimate paradox of vulnerability—Sethe's love is so fierce that it leads her to a devastating choice, one that she regards as an act of protection. Morrison forces the reader to grapple with an impossible question: Is death truly better than slavery? Sethe's vulnerability lies in her belief that she did what was necessary, even as Paul D challenges her.

Exercise: Writing Through Vulnerability

This exercise will help you practice writing from a place of vulnerability, whether you're working on a memoir or a fictional story. Note: please approach difficult memories carefully. If you feel overwhelmed, pause, step away, or skip the memory entirely.

Step 1: Identify a Vulnerable Moment

Think of a moment in your life that feels emotionally significant—a time when you felt afraid, ashamed, heartbroken, or deeply unhappy. It doesn't have to be a major life event; even small moments of vulnerability can be powerful.

Step 2: Write the Scene

Write about that moment in detail. Don't worry about crafting perfect sentences—just try to capture what this was like for you. How did it feel? What were your thoughts? What did you fear or hope for in that moment? How did you behave? What did you say or do?

Step 3: Reflect on the Experience

After writing the scene, take a moment to reflect on how it felt to write from a place of vulnerability. Were there moments when you wanted to hold back? How did you manage those feelings? Did going deeper enable you to feel more connected to your writing? Consider what you initially wanted to withhold—and whether putting it on the page strengthened it. What elements made the scene feel realistic?

Writing Prompts

The following writing prompts will help you write about some of the vulnerable truths you've been carrying. Let them guide you inward and onto the page. At this point, you're writing just for yourself—no pressure, no polish, no audience. Just write.

Exploring Your Own Vulnerability

- Think about something you regret. Write about it with compassion. What circumstances, beliefs, or fears led you to that moment? What version of you made that choice, and why?
- Write about a great loss and what you learned about yourself and the world as a result of it.

Shifting Perspective on Vulnerability

- Revisit an old wound—but tell the story from the perspective of the person who hurt you. How would they justify it? What don't they understand?

- Think about a time when you caused pain to someone who was vulnerable. How do you see that moment now? What can you learn by looking at it from both their perspective and your own? What meaning can you take from that experience?

Fictional Prompts on Vulnerability

- Write about a character who has made a terrible mistake—something they can't take back. Instead of focusing on the aftermath, trace the path that led them there. What were the pressures, fears, desires, or misunderstandings that shaped their choice? Be as compassionate as possible in telling their story. Let the complexity of their humanity show through.
- Your character has been avoiding something for years—until an unrelated accident or event forces them to confront it. What happens?
- Your character is seen as strong and fearless—but someone discovers a small, surprising habit that reveals their insecurity. What is it?

Guided Visualization: A Visit with Vulnerability

Find a quiet, comfortable space. Take a slow, deep breath in… hold it for a moment… and exhale fully. Let go of any tension in your shoulders, your face, and your hands. With each breath, soften a little more and sink into the surface that is beneath you.

Now, imagine a house that exists only in your mind.

You built it yourself. It is a safe place that exists only for you. No one else can see or enter this special house. It's hidden from the world, tucked away in a place where only you can go. And you can access it at any time.

You created this house with comfort and safety in mind. The building may be simple or grand—surrounded by trees, perched on a cliff, nestled in snow, or floating gently above the clouds. Picture this sanctuary that is just for you and where it is located.

Now, step inside your house and notice how the air shifts—as if welcoming you. It knows you. This is a place where you can relax, where you can remember, where you can explore what matters to you. This is a home for your full self.

And because you are safe, truly safe, the stories you've carried—the ones buried, the ones too tender to name—begin to stir. You don't have to force them. Just being here and feeling safe is enough.

You sink into a comfortable chair, feeling it support you in every way. There is nowhere for you to be, nowhere for you to go. Just relax in this house that exists just for you.

With each breath, allow yourself to drift inward—back in time. There's nothing to force. No need to dig. Simply be open, and trust that a moment will arise—a time when you felt vulnerable.

Maybe it was a moment of failure. Maybe you felt unseen or unheard. Perhaps it was the weight of a secret, the sting of rejection, or the ache of loneliness. Maybe it was a time when you wanted to speak but stayed silent. Perhaps someone hurt you, in a small or large way. It was a time when something stirred strongly inside you.

Let the memory choose you.

Once it arrives, don't push it away. Stay with it and observe. Where are you? What's happening? Who is there?

Step inside this version of yourself. Feel what you were feeling. Is there tightness in your chest? A lump in your throat? A weight in your stomach? Do you feel exposed? Small? On the verge of tears? Or maybe it's numbness—something you tried to push away. Whatever arises, let it be there. There's no need to push it down. It's just a memory, and you are safe in this house.

If you become overwhelmed, you can take a break. Otherwise, stay. You are safe.

Now ask: *What was I truly feeling in this moment? What was I thinking? What was I afraid of? What do I still carry from this?*

Breathe into these questions. Let the answers come naturally, without judgment.

Now, look at this past version of yourself with compassion. What were you dealing with? What did you believe back then? What were you trying to do? What pressures were shaping your choices? See yourself clearly—and kindly. You were doing the best you could with what you knew.

If you could speak to that younger self now, what would you say? Offer them what they needed: understanding, reassurance, love. Let them know they weren't alone. Give them the empathy they deserve.

Sit with that. Breathe it in. Let it settle.

The Compassionate Writer

You've carried this long enough. It's time to set it down—not to erase it, but to transform it.

This is your story. It belongs to you. And it's ready to come to the page. You don't need to write it perfectly. You don't need to make yourself look good. You don't need to justify it. You only need to tell the truth. You are not writing to be judged. You are writing to be free.

Now, gently bring your awareness back to your breath. Feel the air moving in and out. Feel the ground beneath you. You are here. You are safe.

Pick up your pen. Or open your computer. Don't overthink it. Just write.

*

In the next chapter, I'll discuss how self-compassion can help you mine your life experiences for material, allowing you to deepen your writing even further.

Chapter 4: From Memory to Meaning: Turning Life into Story

"Stories are the way we understand the world and our place in it."
— Naomi Novik

Why Reflection is Essential for Writing

Storytelling is More Than Experience—It's Meaning

I used to think a dramatic experience was all you needed to create good writing—something scary, traumatic, or heroic. But that's not enough. I once went skydiving with my stepsons, assuming it would make a great story—but it fell flat. Then I realized it wasn't really about jumping out of a plane. The real story was about leaping into a blended family—and how terrifying and exhilarating *that* was. Once I found that deeper layer, the piece came alive.

Even if you write about the most vulnerable moment of your life, it won't truly resonate until you understand what the story is *really* about. There's a difference between simply describing an event and making sense of it. What gives a story its power is the meaning you draw from your experience. This chapter is about revisiting the moments that shaped you and discovering the larger truths behind them.

As the founder and editor of *Chicago Story Press Literary Journal*, I receive hundreds of submissions. Many writers recount personal experiences, often painful ones. But I'm not looking for someone to just tell me what happened—and neither are readers. They want something more. Readers want to know how the experience shaped the writer—how it felt, how they coped, and how it changed them. They want to walk away with something they can carry into their own lives. That's why we read stories: to make sense of our lives and the world.

Joan Didion understood this when she wrote *The Year of Magical Thinking*, a memoir about grief. She didn't just describe her husband's sudden death; she explored how grief distorts logic, how we create alternate realities to survive unbearable loss. Through her reflection and clear, lyrical prose, she showed us something profound about how we deal with sorrow.

In my own writing, I've explored difficult and deeply personal moments. In one piece, *The Inheritance of Truth*, I wrote about being left out of a will. My sister and I were shocked to learn our stepfather—whom we had called Dad for more than forty years—had excluded us. The deeper realization wasn't just the betrayal. It was recognizing how he had always used money to control relationships, drawing people close through generosity. As I reflected, I saw how little I'd really known him. And the real twist? He even left our mother out of his will. That revelation opened my eyes to just how much our family dynamic had been shaped by unspoken financial expectations.

These insights helped me begin to process the shock and pain. More importantly, my story resonated with readers. Many wrote to say they had also uncovered uncomfortable truths about loved ones after they died—and were still trying to make sense of them.

That's what storytelling is about. It's one of the oldest ways we make meaning. Long before written language, people gathered around fires to share myths, lessons, and histories—passing knowledge from one generation to the next. Over time, those oral traditions became epic poems, fables, novels, and films. Whatever the form, storytelling has always served the same purpose: to spark imagination, preserve lived experience, and help us navigate what it means to be human.

Meaning Creates Emotional Depth

When we move beyond recounting events and explore what they meant to us, we invite the reader into our inner world. This is where emotional depth lives—not just in what happened, but in how it felt, what we realized, and how it changed us. Cheryl Strayed demonstrates this beautifully in *Wild*. Although the book follows her physical journey along the Pacific Crest Trail, the real story emerges through her reflections on grief, addiction, and forgiveness. It's her deep insight into her relationship with her mother—and the painful process of confronting her past and coping with her mother's death—that transforms the book from a survival narrative into an introspective memoir.

The same principle holds true in fiction. Celeste Ng's *Everything I Never Told You* begins with the sudden death of a teenage girl, Lydia. At first, it seems like a whodunnit—how did this happen? But the emotional depth comes from Ng's exploration of the family's internal struggles: racial identity, parental pressure, loneliness, and the weight of unmet expectations. Through shifting perspectives and intimate reflection, the novel reveals how each family member's unspoken pain contributes to the tragedy. Like *Wild*, it's not just the events that matter, but the meaning the characters, and the reader, extract from them.

The Compassionate Writer

Using Reframing to Find Meaning in Your Experiences

One of the most powerful ways to transform a personal experience into deeper understanding is through *reframing*. This means stepping back to consider other perspectives, exploring what was truly at stake, recognizing the forces that may have shaped the situation, and trying to understand the emotional experience for you and others. It's not always easy, but it can lead to meaningful insight. Reframing rarely happens overnight, but when you approach memory with curiosity, honesty, and compassion, you begin to uncover not just what happened, but why it mattered.

Jesmyn Ward's memoir, *Men We Reaped*, is a powerful example. Rather than simply telling the story of five young Black men she lost—one of whom was her brother—Ward examines the systemic racism, generational poverty, and family dissolution that shaped their lives and deaths. Although the book is a story of grief, it also offers profound insight into the broader injustices that persist in American society. As a result, she invites the reader into a deeper kind of reflection—not just on what happened, but why. And in doing so, she opens the door for more people to connect with her story.

Some Cognitive Biases that Hinder Reframing

As a psychologist, I know there are certain ways our minds work that can make it difficult to view the past with clarity. One common pattern is that we tend to tell stories that cast ourselves in simplified roles—often as the hero or the victim. And our brains reinforce these narratives through a well-documented phenomenon called *confirmation bias*. Psychologist Raymond Nickerson described this bias as the tendency to notice, remember, and give more weight to information that confirms what we already believe, while dismissing or overlooking evidence that challenges it. So as you reflect on your past, try looking for evidence that complicates your original interpretation. Were you or the other person completely the hero or the victim? What might you have missed or misread?

Another common bias is what psychologists call the *actor–observer effect*. Research by Nisbett and colleagues shows that we tend to explain our own behavior based on external circumstances—"I didn't have a choice," or "The situation made me do it." However, we attribute other people's behavior to their personality or character. This can skew how we interpret both our actions and theirs. When looking back, try to recognize the broader context. What pressures might others have been facing that you didn't see at the time, and how might your behavior have been shaped by more than just the situation?

In a similar vein, we also engage in the *self-serving bias*—the tendency to take credit for our successes while blaming failures on outside forces. This pattern is well supported by research; a meta-analysis by Mezulis and colleagues found that this bias appears across age groups and cultures. It can subtly shape the stories we tell ourselves. For instance, we might downplay our role in a painful situation or justify harmful behavior to protect our self-image. So as you look at your memories, keep in mind that your failures and successes may not be quite so straightforward.

Understanding these biases doesn't mean you've been dishonest—it just means you're human. But recognizing them can help you step outside the old narrative and begin to reframe your past in a way that is more honest and more nuanced.

The Compassionate Writer

How to Reframe

Reframing can deepen your writing. It's not always easy, but there are practices that can support you in the process. Here are some techniques to help you begin.

Start with a Question

Before you begin reframing, it's helpful to consider the question that keeps rising to the surface. Questions can be a powerful way into your story because they give you a focus. Your question might be:

- Why did this happen?
- What was this really about?
- What did this moment reveal about me or about the world I lived in?

These kinds of questions don't just clarify your thinking; they help you move beyond the surface of events. And reframing, at its heart, is about discovery. Starting with a question allows you to uncover the deeper meaning that gives your writing resonance.

Here is an example of an emotional event from my childhood—one I understood a certain way at the time but came to see differently through the process of reframing. This piece was published in a literary magazine and was called *In Her Coat: Echoes of Life*.

> *Example*: One of my most vivid memories is from a Christmas when I was a teenager. My parents had divorced, and my mother had remarried a successful executive. That year, my stepfather gave her a mink coat. She cried when she opened the present, overcome with joy. I was horrified. I assumed the

coat was very expensive, and it represented a departure from her prior life. My father, a professor, lived simply; my stepfather was all about flash: expensive cars, big houses, and now this extravagant gift. I also felt deep pity for the animals whose lives had been taken for that coat.

But when I return to that memory now, I ask myself: What was this moment really about? What did it reveal about my mother and about me and my family?

View from Another Perspective

One of the simplest ways to reframe an experience is to imagine yourself as an impartial observer. Step out of the scene and watch it as if it's unfolding on a stage. What do you notice when you're no longer one of the actors? What details stand out? What patterns or emotions become clearer with distance? This kind of dispassionate view can reveal truths that weren't visible in the heat of the moment.

The other powerful way to reframe is to view the event through the eyes of someone who was there. What might they have felt? What fears, needs, or desires might have been driving their actions? This doesn't excuse harmful behavior, but it helps you understand the full emotional landscape of the scene.

> *Example (continued)*
>
> *As an Observer:* From a distance, I see a teenage girl trying to make sense of her mother's new life with a man so different from her father. I see her caught between two worlds, wrestling with two very

different sets of values: her father's simplicity and her stepfather's extravagance.

Through My Mother's Eyes: I imagine my mother saw the coat as an expression of love and generosity. I also believe she was a bit insecure in the new relationship, and the mink coat represented his love and commitment. In addition, because she grew up in a home marked by significant financial hardship, she likely saw the gift as a form of security—both emotional and material. She may also have believed that others would admire the coat and her new lifestyle.

Through My Stepfather's Eyes: I think he saw himself giving her something spectacular and meaningful—a gift that displayed his affection and his ability to provide for her. Perhaps it was his way of saying she mattered.

Identify the Underlying Conflict

Another way to reframe an event is to find the deeper conflict underneath it. It's easy to get caught up in *what happened* without asking what was really going on beneath. When you look closer, you often find more complexity. Ask yourself: What was truly at stake for me? For the other person? What was I hoping to achieve or protect? What might they have been hoping for, even if they never said it out loud?

Often, the real drivers of a conflict aren't in the words spoken in the moment—they're in the unspoken fears, long-held beliefs, and unmet needs shaping both people's actions.

> *Example (continued):* For me, the conflict was complex. I was upset that my mother was rejecting the values of my father—values that I had internalized and believed in. In some ways, I also felt I was losing the mother I knew. Her transformation into someone else's world created a deeper rift between us.

Describe Your Emotional Arc

Another way to reframe an event is to trace its emotional arc. Our feelings often drive how we act, and they can also serve as signals—clues to what truly mattered to us in a given moment. Consider what you felt *before*, *during*, and *after* the event. Were there shifts along the way—hope turning to disappointment, pride giving way to shame, fear softening into relief? Then ask: What do these emotions reveal about the meaning this moment held for me?

By mapping the changes in your emotional state, you can identify meaning that might otherwise go unnoticed. Some writers may even find it helpful to sketch this emotional arc as a kind of timeline, placing key moments along it to better understand the progression.

> *Example (continued):* Before this occurred, I wasn't close with my mother—she preferred my sister over me. After this event, the emotional distance grew deeper. That mink coat became a painful symbol of her departure from the life I had known with her and my father. I hated when she wore it and, over the years, encouraged her to get rid of it because of what it represented.

The Compassionate Writer

Explore the Other Person's Emotional Arc

It's also important to trace the emotional arc of the other person involved. This perspective not only adds complexity to your story but also builds empathy for them.

> *Example (continued):* That Christmas, my mother was elated. She was starting a new life, and this expensive gift probably felt like an affirmation of her decision to marry him. However, her relationship with my stepfather was complicated—she became disillusioned because he was controlling and not always generous with money. She would later save small amounts from the grocery budget just to have a little spending money.
>
> In this light, the mink coat represented not only her hopes and dreams but also the security she yearned for but never fully achieved. Despite many pleas to get rid of the coat over the years, she never did. It remained a symbol of her longing and the life she wanted so much.

Dig for the Deeper Meaning

When you step back and look at the bigger picture, you often find universal themes—truths about human nature, relationships, or the world—that give the event lasting significance. You may have learned something about yourself or about someone you love (or struggle to love).

> *Example (continued):* My story is about how objects can carry deep emotional significance. That mink

coat came to represent my complicated relationship with my mother and her rejection of my father's simpler lifestyle. It also represented my mother's hopes for love, admiration, and security.

Explore Societal and Cultural Forces

Another powerful way to reframe is to consider the larger societal or cultural forces at play. Some experiences are shaped not just by personal choices but by the influence of class, race, gender roles, generational beliefs, or cultural expectations. When you step back far enough, you may realize the story isn't only about what happened between two people—it's also about the systems, norms, and values that shaped them long before the event took place.

> *Example (continued):* Because my mother had only a high school education, she had limited opportunities to earn the kind of income that would allow her to buy such an expensive coat. She also didn't see the importance of education because she had internalized cultural beliefs that men were supposed to provide financially for women, and that women's role was to care for the home and family. These gendered expectations shaped how she saw herself, her worth, and what security meant to her.

Consider the Readers

Another way to reframe is to step into the reader's perspective. Ask yourself: *What do I want someone to think, feel, or understand as they move through this story?* Being intentional about the emotional experience you create can shape the choices you make—

what details you include, the tone you take, and how you pace the narrative. Your story is not just a personal reflection; it's something you are offering to another human being.

> *Example (continued):* My story is probably one that many people can relate to—the painful distance that occurs between ourselves and the people we love. I want readers to feel the complexity of these emotions—the longing for connection and the heartbreak that occurs when relationships change.

Finding Meaning is Personal

As you reflect on the events of your life, remember that this is *your* story—and the meaning you take from it is personal to you. Two people can live through the same event and draw completely different conclusions. Perhaps you were taken advantage of and now see the red flags you missed. Or maybe you recognize that you were at the mercy of someone more powerful and had no control. Or perhaps you've discovered that forgiveness has helped you heal. Whatever the takeaway, it's yours, and it matters. There is no single "right" way to interpret an experience. What's important is that you do interpret it and go beyond the emotions of the event—to see the larger picture.

Shaping Your Story

Once you've uncovered the meaning of an experience, you can craft a story that brings that to life. If your takeaway is that you should have seen the red flags sooner, weave those flags throughout your narrative. Show the moments you missed them or chose to dismiss them, letting the reader feel the tension of what's coming.

If your meaning is that you truly couldn't have anticipated the harm—and that someone powerful hurt you when you had no control—make that power and lack of control visible in every stage of the story. Build your case so the reader feels the inevitability of the outcome.

If your meaning is about forgiveness, show us what happened, how you struggled afterward, and how forgiveness transformed your perspective. Let the reader see *why* it made a difference and what changed because of it.

To help you move from identifying your takeaway to shaping it into a compelling narrative, it's useful to break the process into clear steps. Below are some steps for you to ensure your takeaway isn't just something you tack on at the end, but a thread that runs through the entire piece, giving it depth.

- **Identify your takeaway:** What deeper meaning have you found in this experience?
- **Decide how it shapes the story**: Is it about missed signs, lack of control, resilience, forgiveness, love, or something else?
- **Choose key moments**: Pick scenes that best illustrate your takeaway.
- **Weave it throughout**: Let the meaning build naturally, not just appear in the conclusion.
- **Show:** Use actions, dialogue, and imagery so the reader experiences the meaning.
- **Check for alignment**: Make sure the scenes and details support the takeaway you want the reader to carry with them.

The Compassionate Writer

Using Personal Experiences to Fuel Fiction

Fiction gives you the freedom to take your own experiences and reshape them into meaningful stories—with new characters, different settings, and even alternate outcomes. Through self-reflection, you can mine your life for the bigger insights and the stories worth telling.

You might be drawn to characters who carry the same burdens you've carried but face them differently. Maybe they make a choice you didn't, or they have an ally or insight you lacked. Or perhaps they stumble through the same situation without the resources you had and end up in a completely different place.

Fiction lets you circle back to unresolved emotions and see them from a new angle. A character can carry your guilt, your unspoken questions, your old fears—yet find resolution through another path. You can rewrite the ending of a painful memory—not to deny what happened, but to ask: *What else might have been possible?*

Even the relationships that haunt you can become part of your stories. Instead of recreating them, you can recast them—shifting power dynamics, changing the point of view, reframing the core question. What was really at stake? What did you believe then, and what do you believe now?

Real life gives fiction its emotional backbone. The truth of the feeling matters more than the facts of the event. When you use personal experience as creative fuel, the goal isn't accuracy—it's emotional honesty.

A friend of mine once had a disastrous marriage. She had just lost her father, and in her grief, she married a good friend who had always cared for her. He was a safe and comfortable choice. They even wed on her father's birthday, which she later realized was a way of holding on to her father. But once her mourning eased, she saw that she had made a mistake. When she wrote her novel, she created a heroine much like herself, on the brink of the same choice—but in fiction, the heroine walked away. The story became about playing it safe versus taking risks, with a clear message for women.

Ocean Vuong's novel *On Earth We're Briefly Gorgeous* is another example of using personal experience to create emotionally resonant fiction. Written as a letter from a son to his mother, who cannot read, the book blends autobiography and imagination in a lyrical, fragmented narrative. Vuong explores the trauma of growing up as a queer, Vietnamese American child in a family shaped by war, silence, and displacement. The novel mirrors Vuong's own life, yet the fiction allows him to deepen, reshape, and explore emotional truths that transcend his life story.

Exercise: Reframing

Try the following ways of reframing to better understand something from your life.

Step 1: View from Another Perspective

Start by choosing a difficult or emotionally charged moment from your life. Then, shift your perspective. Rewrite this as an observer, as if you were watching it from the outside. Then write the perspective of someone who was involved in the situation.

Step 2: Identify the Underlying Conflict

At the heart of every compelling story is a conflict—not just external events, but internal struggles. What was at stake for you and the other person? What were you hoping for, even if you didn't express it? What fears, beliefs, or unmet needs might have been involved?

Step 3: Describe the Emotional Arc

What did you feel before, during, and after this moment? What did your feelings reveal about what this experience meant to you? How do you think the other person felt before, during, and after this moment? What do their feelings reveal about them?

Step 4: Discover the Deeper Meaning

Describe what this story reveals about yourself, others, or life in general. What truth does the story hold for you now?

Step 5: Shape the Story for Connection

What do you want the reader to take away and feel as they read your story?

Writing Prompts

The following writing prompts are designed to help you transform personal experiences into stories with insight.

See Your Experience from a New Viewpoint

- Think of a time when you strongly disliked someone or something they did. Describe a moment in detail, including your reaction. Then, shift perspectives. Describe the person and their actions from their point of view. How do you think they saw themselves and what they did?
- Invent a fictional character experiencing a disappointment. Then rewrite the same scene from the perspective of someone witnessing it—a parent, friend, or stranger. What

assumptions or judgments do they make? What do they get wrong or right?

Identify the Underlying Conflict

- Think of a relationship in your life (past or present) where conflict often arose. Write a scene showing one of those moments. Then reflect: What did each person truly want that wasn't being expressed?
- Write about a decision you avoided making. What was the deeper reason for the hesitation? What would it have cost you emotionally to choose one path over the other?

Trace the Emotional Arc

- Think of a highly emotional situation—a falling out, a reconciliation, or a moment when something in a relationship fundamentally changed. First, trace the emotional arc from your own perspective. How did your feelings shift from beginning to end? Then, step into the other person's point of view and trace their emotional arc.
- Write a scene that starts with your character feeling one strong emotion and ends with them feeling something very different. The shift should happen because of what unfolds in the scene, shown through actions, dialogue, and inner thoughts—not by simply telling the reader. Show this emotional arc over time.

Discover the Deeper Meaning

- Write about a story you've told many times. Now tell it again—but this time, include the part you usually leave out. What new meaning emerges?

- Think back to a major emotional moment in your life and describe it in detail. Now ask yourself: What was this really about? What larger forces—personal, relational, or societal—may have shaped it? What deeper meaning can you take from it now that you have more distance?

Shape the Story for Connection

- Create a fictional scene in which a character's struggle mirrors one of your own. What universal emotion is being expressed? What would you want a reader to understand after reading it?
- Think about the deeper meaning you've uncovered from an event in your life. How can you weave that meaning into the narrative—through scenes, tone, and character choices—so the reader can follow and feel it from beginning to end?

Guided Visualization: The Crystal of Insight

The following Guided Visualization will help you revisit a powerful memory with curiosity and compassion. You may choose to read it slowly and lose yourself in its imagery. You can also record it and listen with your eyes closed, or use this journey in your meditation practice. There is no correct way to do this—only the way that feels right for you.

Begin by finding a quiet, comfortable space. Take a deep, steady breath in... and out.

Again, inhale deeply, filling your lungs with air, then exhale slowly, releasing any tension from your body.

With each breath, let yourself settle into stillness.

Now, imagine standing in a dense, ancient forest. The trees have been growing for centuries, their trunks so wide you couldn't encircle them with your arms. They tower above, their leaves catching a soft golden light that filters down in shifting patterns. A narrow path winds into the distance. As you step onto it, breathe in the cool, earthy scent of moss and damp leaves rising from the forest floor. Feel the gentle breeze brushing your skin, bringing a quiet calm, and the springy earth beneath your feet.

You walk slowly, your steps light and unhurried. In the distance, you hear the sound of a small stream making its way through the forest. A few birds chirp somewhere above you, weaving their songs into the sounds of the forest. The soft light filters through the trees.

The path widens, and the forest thins until it opens into a sunlit clearing. As you enter the clearing, you see a magnificent white marble castle, its towers spiraling high into the sky, glowing in the golden light. This is no ordinary building—the stone walls shimmer faintly, as if they hold a quiet magic. The great wooden doors are slightly ajar, as though they have been waiting just for you.

You ascend the steps and push open the doors, certain that you are welcome here. A vast, candlelit hallway stretches out before you. On either side, large arched doorways line the corridor with doors that are slightly ajar. The marble floor glows faintly, laced with silver-veined patterns and tiny inlays of crystal that catch the light as you move. A tall mirror in a gilded frame on your right hangs on the wall. You see your reflection, but for a moment, you think you glimpse other figures too, distant and shifting, like memories caught in glass.

The air is rich with the faint scent of roses. You wander toward the first room on the left, drawn to its carved doorway. The arch is etched with swirling patterns of vines and stars, and at its center rests a golden handle shaped like an open eye. As your fingers brush the handle, the door creaks open. You step inside.

The circular room is warm and inviting. Candles of every color flicker along the curved stone walls, each flame casting a glow to match its hue—deep crimson, soft sapphire, glowing amber, dark emerald. A grand stained-glass window depicts a crescent moon and a key, its colored light spilling across the floor in slow, shifting patterns, as if the room itself were breathing.

At the center of the room stands a massive crystal ball, resting on a pedestal of carved obsidian. It emits a soft energy, its surface swirling with silver mist. You approach, and as you reach it, the mist within the crystal clears, revealing an image from your own life.

This is a moment when you felt exposed, uncertain, or deeply affected by something outside your control. This was a moment of tremendous emotion.

Where are you? What do you see? What details stand out? Watch this memory play itself out as if you were an outsider, witnessing this moment unfold.

From where you stand today, what do you see that you couldn't see then?

Ask yourself:

- What was at the heart of this moment? Not just what happened, but what made it feel so vulnerable?
- What emotions did you experience beforehand?
- Were there choices you didn't realize you had at the time?
- What role did someone else play in this?

Imagine you could talk to this younger version of you. What do they need to hear? Given what you know now, what would you tell yourself? If you could offer them comfort, reassurance, or wisdom, what would it be?

Let the words rise naturally.

The mist in the crystal swirls again, shifting slightly. This time, it does not show the past—it reveals something deeper. A question forms within the crystal.

- What did this moment teach you?
- How has this moment shaped you?
- If someone else were going through this same experience, what wisdom would you share with them?

The mist shifts once more. Now, the crystal reveals something new. A blank space—a story not yet written. Could this experience be the foundation of a memoir piece or a piece of fiction?

You take a deep breath. Then you turn away from the crystal and step back through the ornate door.

You can return to this castle at any time. As you step outside, the air feels warm and comforting. You walk back down the winding path, carrying more than just memories—you carry wisdom.

With each step, you return to your current life. Take a deep breath. What understanding do you have about a moment from your past? When you're ready, begin to write. Not just about what happened—but about what it means.

Your story is waiting.

*

The next step is learning how to write about others—real or fictional—with the same level of depth, fairness, and insight. Whether writing memoir or fiction, creating characters with empathy makes for better storytelling.

Chapter 5: Writing Real People in Memoir: Balancing Truth with Empathy

"We do not see things as they are, we see them as we are."
— Anaïs Nin

Memoir isn't just about telling your own story—it includes the stories of the people in your life. It can be tempting to paint them in broad strokes, especially when vivid memories reinforce a particular view. But the most powerful memoirs show people in all their complexity and reveal the messy nature of relationships. That's what readers connect with most—not just the pain, but the contradictions.

Telling the whole truth doesn't mean softening it. However, if someone has hurt you and your portrayal reads like revenge, it often falls flat—because no one is purely bad. The same is true for people who've helped you; portraying them as flawless, self-sacrificing saints is neither believable nor compelling. Real people are more complicated than that.

So how do you write about others in a way that honors both your truth and theirs? This chapter explores how to portray real people—especially those closest to you—with empathy, nuance, and fairness. While this chapter focuses on nonfiction, the next will show how these same principles apply to fiction.

Why Empathy Matters in Memoir

Memoir is About More Than One Perspective

Your experience of someone is only one part of a larger story. The people in your life have full histories, motivations, and struggles that don't revolve around you—and some of which you may never fully understand. Writing with empathy means acknowledging that reality.

Empathy doesn't mean excusing harmful behavior. It means looking beyond your own pain to consider the factors that shaped the other person's actions. You can still hold them accountable while recognizing their complexity.

A story that focuses only on someone's failures often feels incomplete. But when you include moments where they tried to connect—even imperfectly—you create a character who feels more human. And if you show the forces in their lives that may have shaped their actions, you add emotional depth. The result is a narrative that feels more honest—and readers are far more likely to connect with it.

A Fictional Example

Below are two examples that show how differently a reader experiences a character when they're portrayed with complexity versus when they're not.

Low Character Complexity: My mother only seemed to want to control me and destroy my happiness. While other kids played outdoors, I was stuck inside. And not only that, she confided in me about all her troubles. I was only a child, and I didn't need her burdens. She was a terrible mother.

This version makes harsh, absolute judgments. It tells us what to think without giving us the space to understand the mother as a person.

Higher Character Complexity: My mother kept me indoors so much, which I hated as a kid. But I realized why—she had lost two children to miscarriages before me, so I was precious. She was painfully shy and didn't have close friends, so she confided in me, which I didn't appreciate at the time. I still think it was too much for a child to carry, but I also see that she didn't have anywhere else to put her feelings.

This version still acknowledges the emotional burden placed on the child, but it adds empathy and reflection. It transforms the mother from a flat antagonist into a complex person, and in doing so, it deepens the emotional impact of the story.

Greater Understanding Can Ease Old Wounds

When someone has hurt you, writing about them with empathy can feel like a betrayal of yourself. However, seeing them more clearly can lead to a more realistic portrayal on the page, and it may help you release some of the pain you've been carrying.

For a long time, I struggled to feel empathy toward my mother when I wrote about her. I judged her harshly because she left my father for a wealthy businessman and was an unreliable parent for most of my childhood. But when I stepped back, I saw her differently. She had her own insecurities. She had little education and didn't believe she could provide the lifestyle she wanted, so she married someone who could. Unfortunately, my stepfather felt threatened by her bond with me, and she found herself caught between us.

Her inability to be the mother I needed wasn't about me—it was about her. In many ways, she was still a child herself. She had always relied on men as protectors, believing the only way to secure the life she wanted was through marriage. When I began to see her not just as a disappointing mother but as a vulnerable person shaped by her own fears and limitations, my perspective shifted.

Through that lens, I found compassion for her. And that changed my writing. More than that, it helped me release some of the pain I carried about our relationship.

What is True?

As you think about your past, it may be tempting to believe in absolute truth—that your memories are precise records of what actually happened. But as a psychologist, I know that memory is reconstructive. When we access memories, we reshape them. And what we remember with absolute certainty may be recalled entirely differently by someone else who was there.

When that happens, we might assume *they're* the one misremembering. But the truth is, it's often impossible to say with certainty who's right. Our minds aren't video recorders; they are storytellers.

Some memoirists recommend sharing your work with others to fact-check your memories. That can be useful—but it's important to remember that their memories are no more reliable than yours. That, too, is a kind of truth.

I believe that memories may not be perfectly accurate, but they hold *emotional truth*—the truth of how something felt, what it meant to you, and how it shaped your understanding of the world. If an event lingers in your mind, even if others don't recall it the same way, it's still worth writing about. Be honest. Don't fabricate or distort. Verify facts where you can. But also accept that truth—especially in memoir—is often personal and a little bit elusive.

The Compassionate Writer

How Our Mind Simplifies Information

One thing I know from studying the human mind is that we tend to categorize things quickly—good or bad, right or wrong, like or dislike. We also tend to simplify people, placing them into fixed categories and associating them with specific memories, which then color how we see them. Once we have a perception of someone, we often focus on the events that confirm that view. This is known as *confirmation bias*, which I discussed in Chapter Four. Psychologist Raymond Nickerson described this as our tendency to notice and recall information that supports what we already believe, while overlooking anything that might challenge it.

Another common tendency is to explain other people's behavior as a reflection of their character. If someone acts selfishly, we're quick to assume they *are* selfish. But when it comes to our own behavior, we're more likely to point to the situation—we were stressed, under pressure, or didn't have a choice. This pattern is known as the *actor–observer effect*, a concept described by psychologist Richard Nisbett. His research showed that we often excuse our own actions based on context while judging others' actions as an indication of who they are.

And if that isn't enough, there's also the *self-serving bias*. This is our tendency to take credit for our successes while blaming our failures on other people or external factors. A meta-analysis by Mezulis showed that this bias is common across ages and cultures.

I mention these patterns because they're pervasive. We all have them, and they shape how we remember and interpret the past. So as you reflect on your life and the people who've shaped it, try to be open to the possibility that your view—while honest—is incomplete. There may be far more to those individuals, and to your own story, than you first realized.

This becomes especially important when you're writing about people you love. Family members, close friends, or partners often play major roles in our stories—and writing about them can stir up feelings of loyalty, pain, or a desire to protect them (or ourselves). That emotional reaction is what makes it so challenging, and it can shape not only what we remember, but also what we choose to write.

Challenges of Writing About Others

Loved Ones Presently in Your Life

Sometimes the hardest people to write about are the ones you love the most. When writing about family members, friends, or partners, you may worry about hurting their feelings or betraying their trust. You may feel torn between telling your truth and protecting them. Empathy can help you navigate this tension by focusing on fairness. Instead of avoiding difficult truths, ask yourself:

- How can I tell this story in a way that acknowledges the positive and negative parts of them?
- What would I want someone to consider if they were writing about me?
- How much does this violate this person's privacy?

If someone you love has made mistakes, try to approach those memories with compassion—for them and for yourself. Ask yourself what might have motivated their behavior. Writing honestly doesn't have to be cruel, and writing with care doesn't have to mean being dishonest.

The Compassionate Writer

However, you might not be ready to extend compassion just yet—and that's okay. Sometimes, you need distance from the pain before you can write about someone.

People Who Are No Longer in Your Life

Writing about people from whom we are estranged or who have passed away can be tough. It's easy to idealize those who are gone or to demonize those we've excised from our lives. In both cases, it's important to look beyond isolated moments of pain or joy and try to see the full person. Here are some ways to achieve this.

- When writing about someone you're estranged from, consider what led to the break. Are there parts of the story you never fully understood? What might their perspective be?
- When writing about someone who has passed away, resist the urge to portray them as perfect. Honoring their full humanity—including their imperfections—creates a more realistic portrayal.

Practical Strategies for Writing with Empathy

Provide a Full Picture of the Person

One common problem in memoirs is reducing people to a single role—villain, hero, or victim. These caricatures are not believable or interesting.

Maya Angelou's *I Know Why the Caged Bird Sings* offers a profound example of how to portray complex people with emotional honesty and nuance. She writes about her childhood experiences of abandonment, racism, and sexual abuse with unflinching clarity—but never reduces those who harmed or failed her to one-dimensional villains. When writing about her mother—who sent her away as a child—Angelou expresses awe, love, and pain all at once:

> "To describe my mother would be to write about a hurricane in its perfect power. Or the climbing, falling colors of a rainbow... I had never seen a woman as pretty as she who was called, 'mother.' Bailey on his part fell instantly and forever in love... he had forgotten the loneliness and the nights when we had cried together because we were 'unwanted children.'"

Rather than offering simple moral judgments, Angelou presents these individuals in their full complexity—capable of both beauty and harm, strength and failure. This emotional depth invites readers not only to witness her story, but to feel the weight of it and to experience the contradictions of the people who shaped her early life.

If you want to bring this kind of understanding to the people in your memoir, try the following:

- List three positive and three negative traits for each major person in your story. Think in terms of contradictions.
- Recall both the positive and negative memories about them. Let the tension between those moments help your portrayal.
- Consider what other factors may have influenced their behavior—trauma, fear, culture, historical context, socio-economic status, gender, race/ethnicity, or beliefs—not just how they felt about you.
- Consider how their desires and objectives might have shaped them.

The Compassionate Writer

- Write scenes that show both their flaws and their strengths. Let readers see the complexity of these individuals through action and dialogue.

Show, Show, Show

Many writers have strong feelings about this issue. Some believe that the only way to tell a story is by "showing" it. *Showing* means revealing character and emotion through actions, dialogue, and sensory details, allowing readers to experience the moment themselves. *Telling* summarizes or explains events or feelings directly to the reader.

I believe in both showing and telling, but many writers lean too heavily on telling. So be intentional. Rather than writing "My sister always made me feel small," let us experience that dynamic through a scene. Maybe she corrected your grammar in front of your friends, or rolled her eyes when you shared an idea, saying, "That doesn't make sense." Describe the raised eyebrow, the condescending smirk, or the way she interrupted you while in mid-sentence. These small details can bring the person to life on the page. Below are two versions of the same story, told in different ways. This is a fictional example and not drawn from my own life.

An Example of Telling

My father was overbearing and never let me make my own decisions. He always thought he knew what was best for me, like the time he insisted I go to his alma mater instead of the school I had my heart set on.

An Example of Showing

"You'll go to Dartmouth," he said, without looking up from the newspaper.

I tightened my grip on the brochure in my lap. "But I've already been accepted to Emerson. Their writing program is—"

He folded the paper with a sharp flick. "You can write anywhere. Dartmouth has history. Reputation."

"I want to study somewhere I feel inspired."

He raised an eyebrow, gave a short laugh, and pushed his coffee cup aside. "You'll thank me later."

That was the end of the conversation. I crumpled the brochure that I'd been carrying around with me for weeks.

You can see how much more immersive the writing becomes when it leans toward showing the character rather than simply telling us about them. When a writer relies too heavily on telling, it creates distance and keeps the reader at arm's length. Aim to do both—but with an emphasis on showing.

Empathy and Boundaries: Knowing What to Share

Although empathy is an essential tool, it's also important to recognize that writing about others can have real-world consequences. Your words may affect the people you write about, especially if they're still in your life. How do you balance the need for honesty with the need for sensitivity? How do you decide what to share and what to keep private?

The Compassionate Writer

Consider the Impact of Your Words

Before publishing your memoir or sharing it with others, take a moment to consider how it might affect the people involved. Will your words cause harm? Will they feel misrepresented? How would you feel if the roles were reversed?

Some writers choose to share their memoir with the people they've written about as a way to stay honest and acknowledge how they've portrayed them. This can help manage the emotional impact of the work—and in some cases, lead to deeper understanding or a stronger relationship.

Ask Yourself Why You're Including Certain Details

It's important to ask yourself why you're including certain details in your memoir. Is it essential to the narrative? Does it help illuminate a key aspect of your experience or character? Are you including it to display a grievance or to hurt someone?

If a scene or memory feels more like revenge writing than storytelling, consider deleting it. Sometimes, leaving certain details out or reframing them with more empathy can make your story stronger, not weaker.

Set Boundaries Around What You Share

Empathy also means understanding your own limits. Protecting your emotional well-being is crucial. You don't have to reveal every painful or private moment. You have the right to set boundaries around your life events. If a memory feels too raw or too personal to share, trust that instinct. You can still explore the emotions or themes connected to an experience without describing it in detail.

This is especially important when writing about sexual assault or trauma. As both a writer and an editor, I believe it's essential to understand how an experience shaped you—and how it made you feel—but it isn't necessary to describe every moment of an assault or traumatic incident unless you choose to.

I personally dislike reading graphic depictions of sexual violence. I'm more interested in how such experiences shape a person's identity, relationships, and overall sense of self. I want to know how people navigate grief, healing, rage, and resilience. That's where the deeper story lives—and where readers most often connect.

Defamation, Lawsuits, and Writing About Real People

If you write something that upsets someone, you may find yourself on the receiving end of a defamation threat or a lawsuit. This can be especially tricky when you're writing about real people, businesses, or institutions.

In North America, it's relatively easy for someone to file a lawsuit, even if their case is weak. Defamation claims are no exception. Fortunately for writers, it's also difficult to prove defamation in court. That said, legal threats, no matter how flimsy, can be stressful and expensive. It's wise to know your rights and responsibilities before you publish.

Defamation, in legal terms, refers to any false statement presented as a fact that harms a person's reputation. When it's written, it's called libel; when spoken, it's slander. To prove defamation, a plaintiff generally must show that:

- The statement was false.
- It was presented as a fact (not an opinion).

- It was communicated to others (i.e., published).
- It caused reputational or financial harm.
- In some cases (particularly for public figures), that it was made with actual malice—meaning the writer either knew it was false or showed reckless disregard for the truth.

Here's an example from my own writing life. After publishing a book about cats, I received a letter from a lawyer threatening a defamation lawsuit. In the book, I had mentioned an apartment building that, according to several sources, was killing stray cats—and I named the building. Shortly after publication, I received a legal notice claiming they were not harming the cats and that they would sue unless I removed their name. I didn't want the stress or expense of a legal battle. I kept the information that the building was believed to be harming cats, but I removed the name. I also agreed not to name them in any future editions of the book.

Would they have won in court? Probably not. But I had to ask myself whether naming them was essential to the story. It wasn't. The heart of the narrative was about the cats and the community's response. Removing the name protected me without compromising what mattered most.

This is the kind of real-world situation writers rarely think about until it happens. So how can you protect yourself while still writing truthfully and powerfully?

Tips for Writing About Real People and Institutions:
- Stick to the truth and be ready to back it up with evidence.
- Avoid presenting speculation as fact. If you're unsure, use phrases like "it seemed," "I heard," or "many people believed..."

- Change names and identifying details when possible, especially if the story is personal and the person is not a public figure.
- Use a disclaimer, such as: "Some names and identifying details have been changed to protect privacy."
- Frame observations of bias as personal perspective rather than assumed fact. For example, "I felt dismissed because I'm a woman" conveys the impact without assuming intent, whereas "He ignored me because I'm a woman" asserts motive and can oversimplify the situation.
- Consult a publishing attorney if your work involves potentially controversial claims.
- Consider errors and omissions (E&O) insurance for extra protection—especially if you're self-publishing or writing investigative nonfiction.

I'm not a lawyer and can't provide legal advice. If you believe you're at risk of being sued for defamation, I strongly recommend consulting with a qualified legal professional. Legal counsel can help you understand current defamation laws and any relevant precedents specific to your situation.

Writing about the real world carries risks, but it also holds great power. When handled carefully, your words can expose injustice, raise awareness, and spark meaningful conversation. The key is to ground your truth in fact and deliver it with clarity and respect.

The Compassionate Writer

Some Famous Examples of Legal Challenges

Authors have long faced legal scrutiny when their work blurs the line between fact and fiction, or when it challenges social, moral, or legal norms. One well-known example is Augusten Burroughs, whose memoir *Running with Scissors* led to a defamation and invasion of privacy lawsuit in 2005. According to *Poets & Writers*, the family portrayed in the book claimed the depiction was not only false and damaging, but that they were easily identifiable. Although Burroughs stood by his version of events, the case was settled out of court in 2007. As part of the agreement, he added a note to the book acknowledging that the family remembers things differently, and agreed to describe it as a "book" rather than a memoir.

In another high-profile case, James Frey, author of *A Million Little Pieces*, faced public and legal consequences when it was revealed that his supposed memoir had been heavily fictionalized. After an exposé by *The Smoking Gun* in 2006 revealed that many details—including time in jail and key events—had been fabricated or embellished, readers filed a class-action lawsuit against Random House, the publisher. The case was settled, and purchasers were offered refunds, though Frey was not personally sued. This controversy reshaped how publishers vet and label memoirs, raising questions about the ethical boundaries of "truth" in nonfiction.

Greg Mortenson, author of the bestselling memoir *Three Cups of Tea*, faced intense scrutiny after a 2011 *60 Minutes* investigation and Jon Krakauer's exposé revealed that key parts of the book were fabricated or exaggerated. As NPR's Neuman reported at the time, questions were raised not only about the truthfulness of Mortenson's stories but also about the finances of his charitable foundation. Mortenson's story of building schools in remote Pakistani villages was called into question, along with allegations of financial mismanagement at his nonprofit, the Central Asia Institute. Following an investigation, Mortenson agreed to repay one million dollars to the organization, though he faced no criminal charges. A class-action lawsuit by readers was dismissed, but the controversy became a cautionary tale about the blurred line between memoir and fiction.

Empathy in Action: Examples from Memoirists

Writing about real people and real events from your life can be incredibly challenging. But approaching your story with empathy and emotional honesty can make all the difference. The most powerful memoirs often reflect a genuine effort to understand others, even in painful or complicated circumstances. Below are a few examples of memoirists whose work resonates deeply because they embraced this approach.

Jeannette Walls' memoir, *The Glass Castle*, described her unconventional and often traumatic upbringing with parents who were loving, creative, and deeply flawed. Walls wrote about her father's alcoholism and her mother's neglect without vilifying them. Instead, she portrayed them as complex individuals who loved their children, even as they failed to care for them. Her empathy for her parents, despite their failings, added depth to her story and allowed readers to see them as multidimensional people.

In *Educated*, Tara Westover writes about her family's extreme religious beliefs, isolation, and the abuse she suffered from her older brother. Throughout the memoir, Westover navigates the tension between love and loyalty to her family and the need to break free from their toxic environment. Even as she exposed painful truths,

The Compassionate Writer

Westover described her family with empathy, showing how their actions were shaped by their own experiences and beliefs. This approach makes her story so powerful.

In The Liars' Club, Mary Karr paints a vivid portrait of her turbulent childhood in Texas, filled with both humor and heartbreak. She described her mentally ill mother and alcoholic father, but didn't strip away their humanity. Karr is irreverent and brutally honest, but her memoir is infused with compassion—even for those who failed her. She captures their contradictions: their wildness, their creativity, their deep flaws, and their great love. Her writing shows that empathy doesn't mean making people look good—it means showing the many sides of people.

Exercise: Behind the Hurt

Consider a person in your life who has hurt you. Instead of focusing only on what they did, take a step back and explore what may have shaped them.

Make a long list of possible influences on this person's behavior. Think broadly:

- Their childhood and upbringing.
- Parental or family dynamics.
- Early and later life experiences.
- Physical or mental health issues.
- Cultural, societal, or religious beliefs.
- Personality traits.
- Financial or social stressors.
- Traumatic experiences.
- Anything else that may have played a role.

Try not to filter or judge—just write down what comes to mind. Once you've completed your list, review it. Identify the three to five most significant influences—the ones that likely had the biggest impact on how they treated you.

Now, write a few paragraphs exploring these influences in detail. How might these factors have shaped the way they saw the world, and how they related to you?

This exercise isn't about excusing hurtful behavior. It's about writing with a depth of understanding for others that makes your work more powerful.

Exercise: Rewriting a Memory with Empathy

This exercise will help you practice writing about real people with empathy.

Step 1: Choose a Memory

Think of a memory that involves a difficult interaction with someone. It could be a moment of conflict, a disagreement, or a time when they hurt you.

Step 2: Write this Memory from Your Perspective

Write a short scene describing the memory from your own point of view. Focus on how you felt in the moment, what was said, what occurred, and how it affected you. Show as much of the scene as possible—use dialogue, actions, and sensory details. Be as honest as you can about your emotions, frustrations, or pain. Don't worry about being "fair" at this stage; just let your voice and feelings come through fully.

The Compassionate Writer

Step 3: Rewrite the Memory from Their Perspective

Now, rewrite the same memory from the other person's point of view. Step into their shoes and imagine how the scene looked through their eyes. How might they have perceived your actions?

Take some time to consider:

- What might they have been thinking or feeling at that moment?
- What fears, beliefs, or assumptions might have shaped their behavior?
- In what ways did their past experiences influence how they reacted?
- Were they trying to protect something, avoid pain, or meet a need?

This step isn't about justifying their actions—it's about humanizing them. See if you can find even a small thread of vulnerability or emotional logic in their response. That's where empathy begins.

Step 4: Reflect on Both Perspectives

After writing both versions, take a moment to reflect. What shifted for you?

- Did seeing the other person's emotional logic change how you understand the moment?
- Is there space for empathy, even if you still feel hurt or conflicted?
- Can you hold both your truth and theirs at the same time?

This step helps move from dual perspective to emotional complexity, which is the heart of compassionate storytelling.

Step 5: Rewrite the Scene with Compassion

Now, write a new version of the scene that holds both truths. This doesn't mean excusing harm or minimizing your feelings—it means writing with emotional honesty and generosity. Show your own experience clearly but allow the other person's humanity to be visible too. Use this version to explore the complex nature of this relationship.

Writing Prompts

Exploring Perspective: Seeing from the Other Side

- Imagine sitting across from a person who hurt you. They're finally telling you their full truth. What do you think they would say? How would you respond?
- Write about a time when someone wasn't there for you in the way you needed. Then reimagine the moment from their perspective: What might they have been feeling or experiencing? What pressures, fears, or limitations might have kept them from showing up for you?

Reflecting on Your Role in the Relationship

- Write a scene where you were the one who caused harm—intentionally or unintentionally. What motivated your actions at the time?
- Describe a moment when you misjudged someone. What assumptions were you making? How would you write that scene differently now?

The Compassionate Writer

Revealing Complexity and Contradiction

- Choose a real person from your life and list three things you admire about them and three that frustrate you. Then, write a scene showing both sides.
- Think of someone who changed your life in both positive and negative ways. Tell their story in a way that reflects both.

Writing with Compassion Without Censorship

- Describe a moment when someone's flaws became clear to you—but instead of judging them, try to understand their struggle.
- Think about someone you have had difficulty forgiving. Without forcing forgiveness, write about what you now understand about their actions that you couldn't see at the time.

Boundaries, Responsibility, and What to Leave Out

- Write a private scene you've never shared with anyone. Keep it broad and don't include every detail. When you're finished, ask yourself: What is the emotional truth of this scene? What does that truth reveal about you, your experiences, or your needs?
- Choose a painful or private memory that you don't want to describe in full detail. Briefly name what happened in broad terms—just enough to orient the reader—then focus on how it affected you emotionally or changed you. Let the emotional truth come through without disclosing more than you are comfortable sharing.

Anne E. Beall, PhD

Guided Visualization: The Mirror in the Glass Pavilion

Below is a visualization designed to help you revisit someone who has hurt you, but with a sense of empathy. Before you begin, take a moment to choose a specific person—someone whom you'd like to feel more compassion toward.

You will be guided to enter a fantastical world where you are completely safe. There, you will look at the person through a magical mirror, seeing them in many ways. This experience is meant to help you understand them more deeply and cultivate compassion from a place of emotional safety.

You can record this and listen to it with your eyes closed, or you can read through it slowly and let yourself get lost in the imagery. If you already have a regular meditation practice, you can also bring the core idea of this exercise into your regular sessions.

Find a quiet place where you can be still and undisturbed. Take a slow, deep breath in… hold it for a moment… and exhale.

Again, breathe in deeply, filling your lungs with calm… and release any tension as you exhale. Let the world around you fade as you settle into this moment. Let your shoulders drop, feeling the weight of your body supported beneath you.

Now, imagine stepping into another world—a quiet, luminous realm far beyond everyday life. This is a place where time moves differently, where the past and present can be seen with equal clarity. The air here feels different: softer, lighter, carrying only a calm, knowing energy. You are transported into a glass pavilion—an open, radiant structure made entirely of clear walls and smooth, polished floors. Above you, the sky stretches wide in soft hues of silver and white.

The Compassionate Writer

You glance around the pavilion, its glass walls and ceiling dissolving the boundary between inside and out. Though sheltered within, you feel surrounded by the landscape—so visible, it feels almost touchable. Beyond the glass, a wide field slopes gently toward a lake, its surface cradled by a dense ring of forest. To the right, a sculpture garden gleams with silver statues, each one catching the afternoon light. Sunlight pours in from every angle, bathing the space in a soft, silvery glow.

You take in this extraordinary glass structure and the different scenes around you. You wonder what the silver sculptures depict, and you glance at the silver light reflecting off the lake that ripples gently.

At the center of the pavilion stands a tall mirror, framed in delicate silver. Its surface shimmers—not reflecting your face, but offering something deeper, something waiting to be seen.

You are safe here.

You are in control.

You approach the mirror when you feel ready, knowing you can step back at any time. The mirror is not here to judge or to harm. It is simply here to show you someone and to help you have empathy for them.

As you step closer, the image in the mirror shifts and blurs. Then, suddenly, you see them—the person who hurt you.

The mirror hums softly, and the image begins to shift. You are no longer seeing just one version of this person—you are witnessing them at different stages of their life. Allow the mirror to reveal a moment from their past. What do you see? Perhaps they are a small child, a teenager, or an adult.

Imagine them in different time periods, in the ordinary moments of life that leave us all vulnerable—being hurt, feeling disappointed, experiencing heartbreak, or sitting quietly in the weight of deflation. Imagine them as what they are—human. With real desires and real fears. With needs they couldn't always express and mistakes they couldn't always avoid. With hopes that sometimes soared and sometimes fell short.

How are you feeling right now? If you're overwhelmed, you can step back and come to this pavilion another time.

The image in the mirror shifts again. You see different memories you have of them. How do they seem? Really look at them. What pressures are shaping them now? Are they carrying wounds from the past? What are they trying to do? Watch different moments of their life.

The mirror shifts once more, reflecting a moment when they hurt you. See that moment clearly. And if you need to, step back from the mirror. Take a deep breath. If it feels like too much, walk away. You can leave the pavilion, stepping out over to see the silver statues. You can always return when you're ready.

If you're ready to continue, look into the mirror again and simply observe. You don't need to excuse their choices, but gently ask yourself: What might have been happening in their life that led them to hurt me? What pressures, fears, or old wounds could have shaped their actions?

When you need to, step back from the mirror again. Take a breath. Leave the pavilion if you wish—walk beside the shimmering blue lake. Toss a few stones into the water. And when you're ready, return to the pavilion and step up to the mirror.

Look into the mirror and ask yourself:

- What did they believe, even if it wasn't correct?
- What were they feeling when they hurt me?
- What did they need that they didn't have?

Imagine what it might have been like to be them at this moment.

Now step back. You don't have to forgive them. But notice how it feels to see them in their full humanity—not only as the person who hurt you, but as someone shaped by their own past. If it feels right, imagine whispering a thought—not of forgiveness if you're not ready, but of recognition. A simple acknowledgment that, like you, they have struggled, they are imperfect, and they carry the imprint of their own history.

The mirror shimmers once more, returning to its original state until all that remains is your own reflection. What has changed? What do you see in your own eyes now? The mirror has shown you something important—not just about them, but about yourself.

Take a deep breath, letting that truth sink into your heart.

You are transported from the glass pavilion to your current life. Take a moment to write. What did you see? What did you learn? Let the words flow freely, without judgment.

*

In the next chapter, I'll shift from real people to fictional characters, exploring how empathy can deepen the way you create characters in fiction.

Chapter 6: Creating Complex Characters in Fiction Through Empathy

"When writing a novel a writer should create living people; people not characters. A character is a caricature." — Ernest Hemingway

One of the great joys of writing fiction is creating entire worlds and people from your imagination. But even in fiction, authenticity matters. Readers connect with characters who think, feel, and act in ways that seem believable. To write characters who resonate, you need to understand them as intimately as you would a close friend—or even yourself.

This chapter explores how empathy brings fictional characters to life. Whether you're crafting a protagonist readers will root for, a villain they'll grudgingly understand, or a supporting character who quietly steals the scene, this level of understanding is what brings them fully to life. It is the secret to creating characters who readers connect with on a deeper level.

Empathy Makes Characters Relatable

When readers understand the reasons behind a character's actions—even when those actions are deeply flawed—they become more emotionally invested in the story. Take Edmund from C.S. Lewis's *The Lion, the Witch and the Wardrobe*. He betrays his siblings by aligning with the White Witch, and at first, his behavior appears selfish and cruel. But as the story unfolds, we begin to see the insecurity behind his choices: the feeling of being overshadowed, his craving for recognition, and his deep sense of being misunderstood. These motivations don't excuse his betrayal,

The Compassionate Writer

but they make it more understandable, which draws readers into his internal conflict and makes his eventual redemption all the more powerful.

Empathy Creates Meaningful Conflict

Conflict is at the heart of great storytelling, but the best conflicts aren't simply battles between good and evil. They're rooted in the clashing motivations, desires, and fears of fully developed characters. Empathy allows you to understand and portray both sides of a conflict with equal depth, so it doesn't feel one-sided, which creates richer tension.

For example, in *To Kill a Mockingbird* by Harper Lee, the conflict between Atticus Finch and the townspeople of Maycomb over his decision to defend Tom Robinson isn't just good versus evil. From Atticus's perspective, it is a moral imperative: he knows Tom is innocent and feels compelled to stand up for justice. From the townspeople's perspective, however misguided, their hostility toward Atticus reflects their fear of social change, their desire to preserve a certain way of life, and their own deeply ingrained prejudices. By showing the humanity, even in the flawed reasoning of both sides, Lee portrays the conflict not as a flat clash of heroes and villains, but as a complex collision of morality, fear, and cultural values.

Empathy Helps Avoid Stereotypes

It's easy to fall into stereotypes, especially when writing characters who differ from you in age, ethnicity, religion, or background. Without realizing it, you might lean on clichés or rely on shallow portrayals. To avoid this, take the time to see each character as a fully developed individual—with their own history, beliefs, fears, and desires—not just as a stand-in for a group or identity. Every character should have a reason to exist beyond moving the plot forward. I explore this issue more fully in Chapter Nine. Stereotypes are cognitive shortcuts that simplify complex information in life. But in writing, they do the opposite of what we want—they flatten characters and strip away the nuance that makes them feel real.

How to Develop Characters through Empathy

To create complex, believable characters, you must understand them as if they were real people. They should feel fully alive to you, complete with quirks, flawed beliefs, private fears, and personal dreams. When you know your characters this well, they often begin to guide the story themselves.

A novelist friend of mine once said that her main character woke her in the middle of the night to reveal how the rest of the book should unfold—and she wrote it exactly that way. The character had become so vivid that they were having actual conversations in her dreams. When your characters feel that alive, your storytelling gains depth and authenticity. Here are some practical strategies to help you reach that level of connection and realism.

Understand Your Characters' Motivations

Every character wants something—whether it's love, power, freedom, revenge, or simply survival. To write them well, you need to understand what drives them and why. What are their goals? Sometimes these goals may seem simple at first. But as you get to know your character, you'll see their desires are often shaped by deeper fears, longings, past wounds, or unmet needs.

The Compassionate Writer

A powerful example comes from Kazuo Ishiguro's *The Remains of the Day*. Stevens, the aging butler, is devoted to a life of dignity, structure, and loyalty—values that have defined his identity. But beneath his unwavering professionalism lies a deep well of repression and regret. In a quiet moment of reflection, he offers a painfully honest glimpse into what truly motivated him.

> "Lord Darlington wasn't a bad man. He wasn't a bad man at all. And at least he had the privilege of being able to say at the end of his life that he made his own mistakes. ...He chose a certain path in life, it proved to be a misguided one, but there, he chose it, he can say that at least. As for myself, I cannot even claim that. You see, I trusted. I trusted in his lordship's wisdom. All those years I served him, I trusted that I was doing something worthwhile. I can't even say I made my own mistakes. Really—one has to ask oneself—what dignity is there in that?"

Ishiguro writes with compassion for Stevens—not to excuse his choices, but to reveal what lies behind them.

Create Flawed Characters

No one is perfect—not in real life, and not in fiction. In fact, the most engaging characters are often the most deeply flawed, because their imperfections make them feel human. When they reveal their fears and vulnerabilities, readers can see parts of themselves reflected in these characters.

One of the most enduring examples of a flawed character is Jay Gatsby in *The Great Gatsby* by Fitzgerald. Gatsby's biggest flaw is his inability to let go of a fantasy. He believes with absolute certainty that he can reclaim his lost love, Daisy, and restore the past. When challenged, he exclaims:

"'Can't repeat the past?' he cried incredulously. 'Why of course you can!'"

That single line reveals Gatsby's longing, his self-delusion, and his vulnerability. Fitzgerald doesn't ridicule him; instead, he invites us to feel the full ache of Gatsby's dream, even as we witness his inability to achieve it. By the end, it's painfully clear that Gatsby can't reclaim his lost love. And yet, we still want his dream to come true. He feels real because he embodies a universal longing: the deep nostalgia so many people carry, and the aching desire to recover what has slipped away.

Use Subplots and Secondary Characters as Mirrors

In fiction, characters are revealed not just through their internal thoughts or relationships, but through subplots and secondary characters. These individuals and events provide contrast and depth, allowing the protagonist's emotional life to be seen from multiple angles.

Imagine a story about Jane, a paramedic who's known for staying calm in every crisis. On the surface, she seems unshakable. But through her relationship with her younger brother, Dylan—an impulsive musician who constantly gets into trouble—we begin to see cracks in that calm. When Dylan lands in the hospital after another reckless night, Jane's anger and fear spill out. Her lectures to Dylan sound less like scolding and more like desperation. Through Dylan, we see that Jane's composure isn't just strength— it's armor. The subplot with her brother doesn't distract from the main story; it reveals the cost of Jane's self-control and deepens our understanding of who she really is.

Secondary characters can also function as foils—individuals who highlight contrasting traits in your protagonist. A selfish friend, an idealistic sibling, or a ruthless boss can illuminate what your main character believes, values, or fears.

Subplots offer another way to reveal depth. A person might be tender with a child but emotionally distant with a sibling. These kinds of contradictions are deeply human. Our behavior changes based on our relationships and situations. Use subplots and supporting roles not just to advance the story, but to reflect and reveal who your main character truly is.

Use External Conflicts to Reveal Character

Characters are often revealed when they're under pressure. External conflict forces them to make choices, take risks, or take a stand. Those decisions—especially when there's something at stake—are what show us who they really are.

Think of a character who refuses to follow an immoral order, even when disobedience carries consequences. Or someone who lies to protect another, only to suffer guilt later. These moments expose not just what a character thinks, but what they're willing to do—and what it costs them.

Fiction gives you the opportunity to show how personality, values, and contradictions emerge under stress. A character may start out self-serving and be forced into responsibility. Another might believe they're brave, only to freeze when it matters most. Whether it's a battlefield, a courtroom, or a family dinner brimming with secrets, conflict reveals the internal complexity behind a character's actions.

Ask yourself:

- What lines will your character cross—and which won't they?
- What beliefs are tested when pressure mounts?
- What internal contradictions are revealed when they're forced to act?

A complex character isn't consistent—they're layered. Let external challenges bring those layers to the surface.

Use World-Building to Reveal Character Through Empathy

World-building isn't just about setting—it's about pressure. The systems, norms, and hierarchies that shape your fictional world also shape your characters. Their beliefs, blind spots, habits, and assumptions are often inherited from the cultures around them. That's where complexity begins: in how a character adapts to, resists, or reinforces the world they live in.

In Margaret Atwood's *The Handmaid's Tale*, Offred's smallest acts of kindness—offering comfort, sharing forbidden words—are charged with emotional risk because the world she lives in punishes connection. Her inner life becomes visible not just through what she feels, but through how bravely she expresses it within an oppressive system.

A well-built world puts pressure on your characters from every direction. A person raised in a rigid society might appear obedient but harbor subversive thoughts. Another may question the rules but benefit from them. These tensions—between belief, behavior, and environment—show us who they are and who they might become.

The Compassionate Writer

Ask yourself:
- What has this world taught your character to believe?
- Where do their instincts align—or clash—with those expectations?
- What do they gain or lose by conforming or rebelling?

Explore Your Characters' Fears

Another way to create engaging characters is to understand their fears. Everyone fears something—whether it's public speaking, rejection, failure, or not being loved. Fear often shapes the decisions people make, the risks they avoid, and the mistakes they repeat.

Gatsby's belief that he can recreate the past is rooted in the fear of losing the identity he has so carefully constructed. Without Daisy and the life she represents, he worries he'll be exposed as an imposter. Recognizing this fear makes his tragic flaw not only believable but deeply moving.

When you uncover a character's core fear and how they try to cope with it, you can portray them with greater compassion. You reveal not just what they do, but why—and that deeper understanding naturally adds tension and plot to your writing. It's what transforms a character from a set of actions into a living, breathing person.

One way to bring fears to light is to consider the memories that haunt them—the painful experiences that have shaped their coping mechanisms and emotional life. For example, a character who was publicly rejected at a school dance might avoid formal social gatherings altogether, fearing humiliation. Memories like this linger, influencing how a character approaches the world.

Anne E. Beall, PhD

Give Major Characters a Moment of Vulnerability

Major characters need moments of vulnerability for readers to truly relate to them. These instances reveal their humanity—moments when their greatest fear comes true, when they make a mistake, or when they feel deep shame.

In *Pride and Prejudice*, Jane Austen offers a powerful example through Elizabeth Bennet. When Elizabeth visits Pemberley with the Gardiners, she dreads the possibility of encountering Mr. Darcy, remembering how harshly she once rejected him. When Darcy unexpectedly appears, Elizabeth is shaken. She becomes acutely aware of her family's lower social standing and of her own conflicted feelings toward him. For a character who is usually confident and witty, this sudden self-consciousness exposes a significant moment of vulnerability.

This scene is powerful because Austen allows readers to witness Elizabeth's private unease—her defenses stripped away, her self-assurance faltering. The woman who once laughed at Darcy now struggles with uncertainty and humility, emotions that make her deeply human and relatable.

As you develop your major characters—the ones who drive most of the plot and action—think about:

- What moment forces them to confront something painful about themselves?
- How does it change them?

The Compassionate Writer

How to Depict Relationships through Empathy

Another way to create engaging characters is through their relationships. Empathy for these complex connections is essential, as they often drive both a character's development and the plot. Whether you're writing a friendship, a romance, or a rivalry, the more deeply you understand that bond, the more authentic it will feel to readers. Here are some tips for writing emotionally realistic relationships:

Show Both Sides of a Conflict

Every relationship is shaped by two perspectives. It's crucial to understand and show both sides. If two characters are arguing, ask yourself: What does each person want? What emotions are driving their behavior? What wounds or misunderstandings are driving this conflict?

Even when one character is clearly in the wrong, try to understand why they're pushing for a certain outcome. Are they acting out of insecurity? Guilt? A desperate need to be seen or heard? When you write from both perspectives, the relationship feels more authentic.

Reflect Real-Life Complexity

Real relationships are rarely all good or all bad—they're messy and full of contradictions. Empathy allows you to capture that complexity, showing how love, resentment, loyalty, and doubt can coexist.

In *Jane Eyre*, Charlotte Brontë creates a relationship between Jane and Mr. Rochester that is passionate yet burdened by secrecy and a clear power imbalance. When Jane discovers the truth about

Rochester's hidden marriage, she is heartbroken. She refuses to stay with him even though she loves him.

> "I care for myself. The more solitary, the more friendless, the more unsustained I am, the more I will respect myself. I will keep the law given by God; sanctioned by man. I will hold to the principles received by me when I was sane, and not mad—as I am now. Laws and principles are not for the times when there is no temptation: they are for such moments as this, when body and soul rise in mutiny against their rigour; stringent are they; inviolate they shall be."

This moment doesn't diminish the love between them. It deepens it. Jane's decision to leave is not an act of rejection, but of self-respect. Brontë shows that love can exist alongside pain, and that true connection sometimes means letting go. By giving both characters depth, Brontë allows readers to experience a relationship that is neither idealized nor simplified, but profoundly human.

Below are some exercises to help you develop your fictional characters.

Exercise: The "Why" Ladder

Choose a character and ask yourself, "What do they want?" Then, ask "Why?" For every answer you give, drill deeper and deeper until you reach the root of their motivation. Here is an example.

- What does your character want? *To get a promotion.*
- Why? *Because they want to prove their worth.*

- Why? *Because they feel overlooked and undervalued.*
- Why? *Because they grew up in a household where they were constantly compared to a more successful sibling.*

Ask as many "why" questions as you need to understand your character. This process will help you uncover the deeper reasons behind their actions, making them more relatable and multidimensional. Note: This exercise is a starting point. Human motivation is rarely simple, so don't be surprised if your character's answers are contradictory and you need to do this exercise a few times to really understand them.

Exercise: Fear Mapping

This exercise will help you flesh out your character by connecting their deepest fears to their behaviors. Start by identifying your character's core fear. It might be fear of abandonment, failure, rejection, losing control, not being loved, or not being enough.

Then, explore how that fear shapes their behaviors:

- How does it influence their choices?
- How does it affect their relationships?
- How does it hold them back—or drive them forward?

Write out the answers to these questions.

Example Character: Maya, a driven 32-year-old architect who grew up in a family that highly valued achievement. Core Fear: Fear of failure

How does this fear influence her choices? Maya always chooses the "safe" projects at work—the ones she knows she can complete successfully. Outside of work, she overprepares for everything—

vacations, events, and dinner parties. She also avoids hobbies she's not good at.

How does it affect her relationships? She rarely opens up about her doubts or insecurities. In romantic relationships, she can come across as cold or distant because she doesn't want anyone to see her struggle. With friends, she's supportive, but deeply competitive.

How does it hold her back—or drive her forward? Maya's fear drives her to work harder than almost anyone else. She's successful but also isolated. She doesn't trust others to see her flaws, and she secretly fears that if she ever fails, people will stop respecting her. That fear stops her from growing emotionally and professionally.

Exercise: The Memory That Haunts Them

Step 1: Identify the Memory

Choose an emotional event from your character's past. Examples:
- A moment when they disappointed or hurt someone.
- A time they felt powerless.
- A conversation they replay repeatedly, wondering if they could have said something different.

Step 2: Write It as a Flashback

Instead of summarizing the memory, immerse yourself in it. Write it as a scene unfolding in real time, with sensory details, emotions, and dialogue. Make it as detailed as possible.

Step 3: Show Its Impact in the Present

Now, create a moment where the memory resurfaces, and show how it influences your character's thoughts and actions in the present.

The Compassionate Writer

Exercise: Write from Different Perspectives

A powerful way to develop empathy for your characters—and make their relationships feel more authentic—is to see the story through different eyes. Try rewriting a key scene from the perspective of another character. What does the antagonist believe about themselves and their actions? What does a minor character notice that the protagonist misses?

This exercise deepens your understanding of everyone involved in the story and helps you create more nuanced, believable characters.

Writing Prompts for Writing Fictional Characters with Empathy

Understanding Motivation: Digging Below the Surface

- Choose a moment when your character makes a bold or reckless decision. Now trace back five layers of "Why?" until you find the emotional reason behind it.
- Write a scene where your protagonist thinks they want something—but by the end, realize it's not what they need. Let their actions reveal their confusion.

Writing Flaws, Fears, and Vulnerabilities

- Write about the moment your character first learned to hide a part of themselves. Who taught them it wasn't safe to be fully seen and what did they learn to hide? Write this as a significant memory.
- Choose your character's greatest fear and write a moment where they unknowingly cause it to come true.

Use Subplots and Secondary Characters

- Write a scene where a major event (a wedding, illness, job loss, or death) happens to someone *other than* your protagonist. Show how your protagonist's reaction reveals something about who they are—what they value, what they fear, or what they can't admit to themselves.
- Choose a background character (bartender, teacher, driver, etc.) and write the scene where they finally snap. What truth have they been carrying in silence?

Messy Relationships: Exploring Push and Pull

- Write about a character who leaves a relationship out of love, not resentment. Show their longing and grief, not just the goodbye.
- Write about a relationship where contradictory emotions coexist. It could be a mix of love and betrayal, grief and hope, anger and tenderness, or another set of conflicting feelings. Show how these emotions shape their relationship over time. How do they influence one or both of the characters?

A Past Memory

- Choose a memory your character avoids. Now write a scene where something in the present forces them to relive it.
- Write about a memory your character is trying to recreate. Then show what happens when they try to bring it back to life. How does the attempt affect them emotionally? Does it bring comfort, disappointment, insight—or something unexpected?

Guided Visualization: Entering Your Story and Meeting Your Characters

The following visualization is designed to help you meet your characters and get to know them more deeply. You'll visit with them and have a conversation to better understand what makes them tick. You can record this and listen to it with your eyes closed, or you can simply read through it and immerse yourself in the imagery. If you already have a meditation practice, you can also bring this journey to your mat and explore it there.

Find a quiet space where you won't be disturbed. Take a deep breath in... and out.

Again—inhale deeply, feeling your chest expand, the air as it enters... and exhale slowly, releasing the weight of any current concerns. Let your body sink into the surface you're on, let your shoulders relax, and feel your body getting heavier and heavier.

Now, imagine a soft glow flickering in the distance—a shimmer gently calling to you. As you focus on it, the glow sharpens into a radiant portal just ahead. Its edges ripple like water, and at its center, colors spiral in slow motion—vivid blues, deep violets, threads of gold and emerald weaving together.

You float effortlessly toward this portal. You feel weightless as you drift toward the swirling colors. You are relaxed, knowing that you are going to a place where you need to be.

As you get closer, you feel the hum of the portal—like a vibration deep in your chest, calm and reassuring. The swirl of colors draws you in as you enter a tunnel of golden light.

The air is warm. You drift deeper into the tunnel. And then you touch down. The ground beneath your feet is solid.

You've arrived—in the heart of your own story. This place, this world, is one you've created. Look around and take in your surroundings.

Now listen... You're not alone. Footsteps echo nearby. Then, stepping forward, your protagonist appears. They study you with curious, knowing eyes. Somehow, they recognize you—even though you've never met.

Take a moment to really see them. Notice the details: their posture, their clothing, the expression on their face. Let the silence hang for just a beat. Then they speak. "You finally came."

You now have an opportunity: to speak with your character.

You ask, "How are you?"

They pause. "You should know... but I'd really like to talk. I want you to understand me better."

Take a deep breath—and begin the conversation. Ask them:

- "What do you want most in this world?"
- "What are you afraid of?"
- "What have I misunderstood about you?"
- "What do you wish I would let you do?"

Listen closely. Let the conversation unfold naturally. Now, ask them one final question. "What is your biggest secret?"

Watch their reaction. Their answer may change everything. Then, there is a shift in the air that causes you to turn. Another character enters the space.

Your antagonist has arrived and your protagonist vanishes.

Now, focus on your antagonist. How do they carry themselves? What do they look like? What expressions do they show?

The Compassionate Writer

Now is your chance to understand them as a person in their own right. Ask them:

- "What do you most want?"
- "What drives you to act the way you do?"
- "What would you like me to know about the other characters?"
- "What do you wish I would let you do?"

Listen carefully to what they tell you. As you take in everything, you feel a shift in the air. The golden light from before returns, swirling around you.

Your time here is ending.

Your protagonist reappears and both characters watch you, knowing you must leave. But before you go, one of them steps forward and gives you a final message. This is a gift from your story, a truth you need to know. What is this message?

The golden light envelops you once more, and before you can react, you are lifted from the world, weightless, and traveling back through the tunnel.

You land gently back in your own life. You take a deep breath while the voices still linger in your mind. You have learned something.

Take up your pen or sit at your keyboard and write down everything—the world, the characters, their words, their secrets. Your story is waiting. And now, you are ready to tell it.

*

In the next chapter, I'll explore how to write conflict with compassion, balancing the emotional truths of all sides to create great stories.

Chapter 7: Writing Conflict with Compassion

"Nothing moves forward in a story except through conflict." — Robert McKee

Conflict is what drives stories forward. Without it, stories have nowhere to go, characters have nothing standing in their way, and readers lose interest. No one wants to read the following story:

Jen was born into a perfect family. She had an easy life, and she died at an old age.

That's boring.

But tell me Jen was born into a family where her sister Mary constantly tried to undermine her, where they battled beneath the surface, but never openly. Now you have something interesting. Tell me that Mary had an affair with Jen's fiancé before the wedding, and now you have my full attention.

Although it's easy to think of conflict as a fight where one side wins and the other loses, the most engaging conflicts are written with a deep understanding of both sides. When you approach conflict this way, you move beyond simple "good vs. evil" or "hero vs. villain" stories into more realistic territory—where readers can see the situation in its full complexity and the humanity of each character.

In this chapter, I'll explore how compassion can shape conflicts that not only drive your story but also resonate with readers.

The Compassionate Writer

Why Compassion is Essential for Writing Conflicts

Compassion Illuminates the Underlying Emotions

Most major conflicts, at their core, are emotional. Even conflicts such as two armies at war or a courtroom battle are ultimately driven by emotions like fear, love, anger, jealousy, and the desire for control or freedom. Writing scenes well means understanding these underlying emotions and showing how they shape different characters' actions and decisions.

For example, imagine a courtroom battle between two neighboring families—one wealthy, the other less so. The wealthy family has installed an enormous sculpture in their backyard, which the other family claims blocks their view of the lake. What seems like a simple property dispute is charged with deeper emotion: the less wealthy family feels their neighborhood is being transformed by money and power, eroding the sense of place they've known for years. The wealthy family, on the other hand, feels unfairly targeted—convinced the others are acting out of jealousy and a desire to control them. At its core, this conflict isn't really about the sculpture; it's about both families trying to reclaim a sense of agency over their home.

Compassion Creates Believable Stakes

The best conflicts are ones where no one is entirely right or wrong. Both sides have their own fears, needs, and desires, which make sense to them. Both believe their actions are justified. This complexity raises the stakes because readers can see how much each character has to lose and how difficult the resolution might be.

Think back to Jen and her sister. Mary slept with Jen's fiancé before the wedding—an act that makes it easy to cast Mary as the villain and Jen as the victim. But dig a little deeper, and the story becomes far more complicated. What if Jen had stolen the love of Mary's life several years ago? What if Jen's fiancé had previously dated Mary, and old feelings were never fully resolved? What if Mary struggles with depression and believes she'll never find lasting love, so watching Jen get married doesn't just spark jealousy, but a deep, aching sense of loss? And what if Mary, despite sincerely trying to repair the relationship, has been met only with silence or rejection?

Suddenly, the story isn't just about betrayal. It's about heartbreak, loneliness, resentment, and hope. Many people can relate to these feelings and can empathize with both sisters, even when they make painful choices.

How Our Mind Simplifies Conflict

Because the world is complex, we often try to make sense of conflict by simplifying it—labeling people as either right or wrong. This impulse becomes even stronger when the conflict involves someone from our own group versus someone outside it. Psychologists call this *ingroup bias*—the tendency to favor those who are similar to us in race, gender, nationality, beliefs, or background. Conversely, *outgroup bias* refers to the tendency to view those who are different from us more negatively, often seeing them as less trustworthy, less capable, or less deserving of empathy.

Henri Tajfel and John Turner, pioneering social psychologists, demonstrated how easily these group distinctions form. They showed that even arbitrary group assignments (like being told you're on the "blue" versus the "green" team) can lead people to favor their own group and discriminate against others. Further research has shown that ingroup favoritism and outgroup derogation can shape everything from personal relationships to political beliefs and cultural narratives.

When writing about conflict—especially between people from different social, cultural, or demographic backgrounds—it's important to be aware of these biases. As writers, we need to look beyond labels, affiliations, and assumptions, and to see the full humanity of each person involved. That doesn't mean pretending there's no harm or wrongdoing. It means allowing for complexity: recognizing that people act from fear, pain, longing, or misunderstanding—not just malice.

Types of Conflict and How to Approach Them with Compassion

Conflict has traditionally been described in a few well-known categories: *person vs. person, person vs. self, person vs. society*, and sometimes *person vs. nature or the supernatural*. I will focus on the first three—interpersonal, internal, and societal—because these are the ones where compassion for the characters makes the greatest difference.

Interpersonal Conflict (Person vs. Person)

Interpersonal conflict is one of the most common types, whether it's an argument between friends, a power struggle between rivals, or a clash between lovers. To write this type of conflict well, you need to fully understand both sides of the disagreement. Why does each character feel the way they do? What is each character trying to do, and why does this conflict upset them so much? What lies underneath this conflict? What past experiences or fears are influencing them?

Practical Tips

- **Write from Both Perspectives**: Even if your story is told from one character's point of view, try writing a scene from the other person's perspective. This will help you understand their motivations and emotions, even if they're not explicitly stated in the story.
- **Show the Emotional Build-Up**: Conflict rarely comes out of nowhere. Show the moments leading up to the argument, including the small frustrations, misunderstandings, or fears that escalate into full-blown conflict.

In *Pride and Prejudice*, Elizabeth Bennet and Mr. Darcy's conflicts are rooted in miscommunication, incorrect perceptions, and pride on both sides. Jane Austen doesn't present either character as wholly right or wrong; instead, she allows readers to see their vulnerabilities, making their eventual resolution even more satisfying.

In my own life, I saw this in my marriage that ultimately disintegrated. It would have been easy to cast my ex-husband as the "Disney Dad" and myself as the parent who made the hard calls, since we often disagreed about how to manage the children. At first, I wrote about these conflicts with anger, but over time I began to see a bigger picture: his more laissez-faire approach came from a childhood where feelings weren't discussed and problems weren't confronted, while my stricter style reflected my family background. Recognizing how our different upbringings had shaped us helped me view our battles as the painful collisions of two people carrying very different histories and expectations.

The Compassionate Writer

Internal Conflict (Person vs. Self)

Internal conflict arises when a character struggles with something within themselves such as fears, doubts, or competing desires. Writing this kind of conflict with compassion means exploring your character's vulnerabilities without judgment. Rather than framing their struggles as flaws, show them as a natural part of being human.

Practical Tips:

- **Identify the Root of the Conflict**: What does your character want, and what is holding them back? Is it fear of failure? Guilt over past mistakes? A lack of self-worth? Understanding the root cause of their internal conflict helps you write it with empathy.
- **Consider Their Past**: What role does the past play in this internal conflict? Were they shaped by someone influential? Did their childhood experiences leave them with fears or desires that now drive their behavior? What past events or relationships have planted the seeds of this inner struggle?
- **Show Moments of Self-Understanding:** Even if your character is struggling, include times where they recognize their own pain, question their behavior, or glimpse the possibility of change. These moments make the emotional journey feel authentic and help readers connect more deeply to the experience.

In *The Catcher in the Rye*, Holden Caulfield's internal conflict revolves around his fear of growing up and his deep-seated grief over the death of his brother. J.D. Salinger portrays Holden's struggles in a way that makes them deeply understandable. Even when Holden behaves in frustrating or self-destructive ways, readers can still feel his pain and longing beneath the surface. Salinger doesn't excuse Holden's actions, but he invites readers into Holden's world so they can connect with him, making his story resonate on a deeper level.

Societal Conflict (Person vs. Society)

Societal conflict occurs when a person is struggling with the world around them—whether it's due to systemic oppression, cultural expectations, or clashing ideologies. Writing this type of conflict well involves showing the complexity of the societal forces at play, as well as the personal stakes for an individual.

Practical Tips

- **Humanize the Opposition**: Even if your character is fighting against an unjust system, show the human side of those who uphold it. For example, a guard enforcing oppressive laws might be driven by fear of losing their job or a sense of duty, rather than cruelty.
- **Highlight the Emotional Cost**: Societal conflict often takes a toll on your character. Show how their struggles affect their relationships, self-image, and sense of hope. This makes the conflict feel more personal and urgent.

In *The Handmaid's Tale*, Margaret Atwood portrays Offred's conflict with an oppressive society that controls women's bodies. While the regime is undeniably tyrannical, Atwood also shows the human side of those complicit in the system, such as the Aunts who enforce the rules not simply out of malice, but because of fear, indoctrination, or the belief that obedience is the only way to survive. This portrayal makes the conflict more emotionally complex. Readers not only witness the brutality of the system but also the ways people adapt to survive within it. By showing how societal oppression can twist human behavior, Atwood deepens the emotional impact of Offred's struggle and makes her resistance feel even more courageous.

The Emotional Journey of a Conflict

Conflicts rarely erupt out of nowhere. Emotions often build quietly over time—through misunderstandings, disappointments, or unspoken feelings. Good writing captures not just the moment of explosion, but the emotional buildup that leads to it. This is called the *emotional journey*.

I'll discuss the emotional journey in greater depth in the next chapter. For now, start by considering the emotional landscape of your conflicts: what feelings simmer beneath the surface early on for both sides? How do they escalate? What changes after the conflict peaks? And what emotions linger afterward?

Writing Compassionate Resolutions

When you depict conflicts, you'll eventually need to resolve them. Resolution doesn't mean tying everything up neatly or forcing a happy ending. But it does mean offering some kind of shift—whether it's learning, acceptance, or a deeper understanding. A strong resolution should feel truthful and earned. To write resolutions with compassion, consider the following approaches.

- **Acknowledge complexity.** The most satisfying resolutions recognize that conflicts rarely have simple answers. Show growth or understanding, even if wounds aren't fully healed.

- **Show reconciliation through small moments.** A flicker of vulnerability, a softened voice, an awkward apology, or the choice to stay instead of leaving can feel more authentic than a grand gesture.
- **Depict unresolved outcomes with honesty.** Resolution doesn't always mean fixing everything. Sometimes it's setting boundaries, recognizing limitations, or finding peace within. Show how characters have been changed by the conflict, even if reconciliation never comes.
- **Highlight growth or transformation.** Readers are drawn to stories that reveal how people change. Show how the conflict leads to new awareness, deeper concern for another person, or a broader understanding of life.

In *To Kill a Mockingbird*, Harper Lee offers a compassionate resolution—one that doesn't tie everything up neatly but still feels emotionally truthful. Tom Robinson, the Black man unjustly convicted of rape, is killed while trying to escape prison. Bob Ewell, the father of the woman who falsely accused Tom, seeks revenge and attacks Scout and her brother, Jem. In the struggle, Ewell is killed, and Jem is carried home by Boo Radley—their reclusive neighbor who had long been misunderstood and feared. In the final scene, Scout walks Boo home. Standing on his porch, she imagines the world from his perspective for the first time. That quiet act of empathy is what makes the resolution feel earned and deeply human.

The following exercises are designed to help you use compassion to create compelling, emotionally resonant conflicts.

The Compassionate Writer

Exercises

Exercise: Explore an Interpersonal Conflict

Writing about conflicts from your own life can be especially challenging. It's easy to view the other person as the problem and to overlook their perspective. That's the nature of conflict: we believe we are right, and they are wrong. This exercise will help you explore each perspective more fully—even if the conflict you're writing about is fictional.

Step 1: Write your perspective (or your character's perspective) on the conflict. Describe it in detail, including why you or your character believes they are "right."

Step 2: Explore the emotions behind this perspective. What feelings are driving it? What past experiences or fears might be influencing the way you/your character see the situation?

Step 3: Now step into the other person's shoes. Write their perspective. Why do they believe they are right? What emotions are they feeling? How might their past experiences shape their view of the conflict?

Step 4: Using what you've uncovered, write a short dialogue or scene that shows both perspectives. Let the complexity of the conflict emerge naturally through this interaction.

Exercise: Explore an Inner Conflict

Internal conflict often feels like a tug-of-war between different parts of ourselves or within a character. This exercise will help you explore the complexity of an internal struggle.

Step 1: Identify a major internal conflict for yourself or for a character. (For example: a desire for independence but a fear of being alone, or a desire to speak the truth but a fear of hurting someone.)

Step 2: Imagine these conflicting parts as two separate characters. Write a short dialogue between them. Let each side express what it wants and what it fears. Try to give each side equal weight and dignity, even if one side feels "irrational" or "wrong."

Step 3: Reflect on what this internal conflict reveals. What emotions are driving each side? What past experiences might have shaped these fears or desires?

Step 4: Write a brief paragraph showing a moment of self-understanding. This could be a moment when you (or your character) recognize the conflict for what it is, make a difficult choice, or take the first step toward healing.

Exercise: Explore the Personal Side of a Societal Conflict

This exercise will help you write about a societal conflict by connecting the personal and the societal aspects.

Step 1: Identify a societal conflict you (or your character) have faced or are facing. For example, discrimination, racism, sexism, navigating cultural expectations, facing political oppression.

Step 2: Write a paragraph about how this societal force affects you or your character's daily life. Focus on small, concrete examples such as an interaction, a missed opportunity, a silent burden.

Step 3: Write a paragraph about how the larger system justifies or perpetuates the conflict. What are the forces—laws, beliefs, traditions—that create or reinforce the injustice? Write about people who, despite good intentions, help sustain this system and show their perspective and what motivates them. How can you understand their behavior without excusing the harm?

The Compassionate Writer

Step 4: Reflect briefly: How does seeing both the personal impact and the systemic forces, along with the human motivations behind them, deepen your understanding of the conflict? Where might compassion fit into telling this story?

Exercise: Mapping the Emotional Arc of a Conflict

This exercise will help you map the emotional journey of a conflict.

Step 1: Identify the Conflict: Choose a key conflict you're writing about. Briefly describe who's involved and what's at stake.

Step 2: Track the Emotions: Focus on the emotions of the person (or people) involved in the conflict. Some writers like to draw a simple line on a piece of paper to chart the emotional journey of a character, marking how feelings rise and fall throughout the story. For this exercise, identify the main emotions at three points:

- Before the conflict (What feelings were simmering beneath the surface?)
- During the conflict (What emotions erupted or shifted?)
- After the conflict (What feelings lingered, changed, or deepened?)

Step 3: Reflect: Looking at the emotional arc, what changed for the person (or people) emotionally? How might this emotional shift be shown in your writing?

Writing Prompts for Writing Conflict with Compassion

Writing conflict with compassion asks you to delve into the emotions, histories, and needs that drive people's actions. The following prompts are designed to help you explore conflict in all its forms: internal, interpersonal, and societal.

Interpersonal Conflict

- Describe a real conflict from your life. What underlying beliefs are driving the conflict on both sides? How much of this tension stems from the feeling that one person doesn't value or respect the other? What might each person need or be trying to protect?
- Write a scene where one character confronts another, believing they've been wronged, but leave clues that their assumptions are incomplete.

Internal Conflict

- Show a character caught between two people they care about. What internal tension does this create, and how do they navigate it?
- Show a character enforcing a rule they privately disagree with. What do they risk by questioning it? What, if anything, cracks their compliance?

Societal Conflict

- Write a scene between two characters on opposite sides of a power structure (teacher/student, police/civilian). Let both be wrong and right.

The Compassionate Writer

- Create a conflict between a person and society. What does the individual misunderstand about the society they're opposing? What does the society misunderstand about the individual? Show how these misunderstandings deepen the conflict.

Emotional Journey of Conflict

- Take a conflict and map the key emotional moments: What feelings were simmering beneath the surface before the conflict? What emotions erupted during it? What lingered afterward? Show the conflict, weaving these emotions into both small moments (glances, gestures, tone) and larger actions (choices, turning points).
- Write a scene showing a slow emotional buildup. Don't write the actual argument—just the subtle hurts, misunderstandings, or disappointments that made the conflict inevitable.

Compassionate Resolution

- Write about a time in your life when you could not reconcile or resolve a conflict in the way you hoped. What did you learn from the experience? How did you eventually find some form of resolution—whether through acceptance, distance, forgiveness, or growth? Describe the conflict, your emotions, and the steps toward resolution in detail.
- Write a reconciliation scene where no one apologizes, but both people take a small, vulnerable step toward healing their individual wounds.

Anne E. Beall, PhD

Guided Visualization: The Sanctuary of Listening

This visualization will help you explore a conflict with greater compassion. You will enter the Sanctuary of Listening—a place where both sides are heard and understood. If you are writing about an interpersonal conflict, imagine two people. If you are exploring an internal conflict, imagine two sides of yourself. If you are writing about a societal conflict, imagine two people who embody each perspective of this struggle.

Find a quiet, comfortable space. Take a deep breath in... hold it... and exhale slowly. Again, inhale deeply, filling your lungs with calm... and exhale, releasing any tension. Let your body soften. Let your mind quiet. Let your heart open.

Now, imagine yourself walking along a sandy path that runs beside the sea. To your left, waves roll steadily toward the shore. Ahead, set just above the beach, rises a graceful white marble building. A wide, grey veranda made of polished wooden planks faces the water. Bougainvillea, heavy with bright pink blossoms, climbs along the walls of the building and sways in the breeze, framing it with color.

The entire seaward side of the building is glass from floor to ceiling, so clear that the ocean and sky are reflected in its surface. You continue around to the far side, where two tall driftwood doors await. Their polished wood bears the natural grain and knots shaped by the sea. The metal handles are cool and smooth beneath your hands. You pull the doors open.

As you step inside, quiet envelops you. The driftwood doors close softly behind. In front of you is a wide, open room with a glass wall offering an expansive view of the sea. The horizon stretches

The Compassionate Writer

endlessly, the water shifting from deep blue to shimmering silver as the light changes.

The interior is airy and light. Grey marble floors flecked with black and white gleam beneath your feet. High above, wooden beams curve like the ribs of a ship—strong and elegant. Three comfortable chairs face the wide window.

A faint breeze carries the scent of salt and the freshness of open water. To your right, a panel of polished wood bears an inscription, the letters glowing softly in the shifting sunlight: *"Understanding is always possible when we truly listen."*

You pause and let the words settle within you.

This is the Sanctuary of Listening.

You are guided to the front of the room and take your place in the middle chair. As you gaze out at the sea, two figures appear and greet you—these may be versions of yourself, characters from your story, or voices of opposing perspectives.

The first person begins to speak as they explain their side of the conflict. They tell you how they feel, what burdens they carry, why they believe what they do, and what they want.

You listen and consider: what is it that they *truly want*—it may not be what they say.

You let their story settle, the way the sea calms after a wave. You breathe in the salty air and notice the ocean's vast horizon, holding their perspective in your heart.

Now, the second person speaks as you listen carefully. They tell you how they feel, why they believe what they do, and the burdens they carry. Their words carry the same story but shaped by different experiences. Their truth feels distinct, yet no less real.

You sit in stillness. Both stories echo softly within you. Neither side is entirely right, and neither is entirely wrong.

What do *you* believe about this conflict?

From this sanctuary, you speak with clarity and compassion. You see what each side cannot yet see. You tell them what each side feels and what each one truly wants—it may not be what they have stated.

They listen carefully to what you say. They see the other side slightly differently. You see understanding begin to grow between them.

Take a deep breath in… and exhale slowly. Feel the ocean begin to dissolve as you return to your present environment.

*

In the next chapter, I'll explore how compassion extends beyond the page, shaping the way your writing connects with readers and the responsibility you carry as a storyteller.

Chapter 8: Emotional Journeys: How to Craft Stories that Touch the Heart

"I've learned that people will forget what you said, people will forget what you did, but people will never forget how you made them feel." — Maya Angelou

Why Readers Crave Emotional Journeys

Think about the last piece of writing that truly moved you. You might not remember every detail of the plot, but you remember how it made you feel. Maybe you cheered for the hero, held your breath during a risky choice, or cringed when they did something foolish. It wasn't just a story—you went on an emotional journey.

Those feelings didn't happen all at once. They were built gradually and intentionally, layer by layer, over the course of the story. That's because emotions rarely arrive fully formed. Love might begin as curiosity, grow into fascination, and eventually swell into something overwhelming. Grief doesn't start and end with a funeral; it often begins in denial, lingers as a dull ache, and resurfaces unexpectedly—a familiar scent, an empty chair, a certain song. A great story captures that emotional evolution.

And the reader plays an essential role in that process. They bring their own memories, relationships, and emotional landscapes to the page. They fill in the spaces you leave open—sometimes seeing themselves in your story more vividly than you ever imagined. In that way, they aren't just observers; they're collaborators.

Crafting this kind of emotional journey isn't easy—especially when you're working through your own complex feelings about people or events in your life. But whether you're writing fiction or memoir, the goal is the same: to create moments that feel emotionally true and leave just enough space for the reader to walk alongside you.

I once wrote about my emotional journey involving my mother—specifically, my disappointment that she hadn't been the kind of maternal figure I needed. But near the end of her life, while she was on heavy morphine, she began singing a whimsical song about dancing bears—joyful, unfiltered, almost childlike. In that moment, I realized she had never really grown up. I had spent years expecting mothering from someone who simply wasn't capable of giving it. With that understanding, I forgave her—not just for the ways she had let me down, but for the ways I had misunderstood her.

The Reader's Emotional Journey: Why We Feel What We Feel

So why do readers feel strongly in response to some pieces of writing? Often, it begins with *sympathy*—a feeling of concern or sorrow for a character's situation. But stories that stay with us go deeper. When readers begin to see something of themselves in a character's struggles, hopes, or flaws, that sympathy deepens into identification. And through that identification, empathy emerges. There's an important distinction: sympathy means feeling for a character, while empathy means feeling with them—experiencing their emotions as if they were your own. It's empathy, built on identification, that gives stories their greatest emotional power.

It's not that readers have lived the exact same lives as the characters or know people just like them. Rather, stories tap into something universal. A character might face loss, feel misunderstood, or fall in love. The circumstances vary, but the emotional experience is relatable.

In *The Book Thief* by Markus Zusak, Liesel Meminger suffers profound loss from the very beginning: her brother dies beside her on a train, and her mother disappears soon after, likely a victim of the Nazis. When her brother dies, she steals her first book—an act that quietly signals the start of her transformation. As she adjusts to life with her foster family, the trauma of those early losses lingers.

Readers first feel sympathy for Liesel—a child navigating grief in a violent, unstable world. But as the story unfolds, her quiet acts of rebellion and her growing moral awareness invite identification. That awareness expands as she begins to grasp the horrific acts committed by the Nazis. Many readers recognize her longing to belong, the confusion of coming of age, and the heartbreak of losing someone too soon. Through that recognition, sympathy deepens into empathy: we don't just feel sorry for her—we begin to feel *with* her. These emotions—her fear in the bomb shelter, her guilt over surviving, and her awe at the power of language—resonate as if they were our own.

An Emotional Hook

Crafting an emotional journey starts with identifying an emotional hook—something that resonates deeply with the character you're writing about (or with you, if you're writing memoir). This hook is the spark that ignites the story. It grabs the reader's attention not just because something is happening, but because something is at stake emotionally.

An emotional hook often stems from a need, a wound, or a longing that the character has at the beginning of the narrative. It could be a desire for connection, a fear of abandonment, a need for forgiveness, or the ache of unresolved grief. Whatever form it takes, it creates an emotional question that drives the narrative forward—questions like: Will I be loved? Can I belong? Am I enough? The story becomes the character's attempt to answer that question, often without realizing they're asking it.

In my essay about my mother, the emotional hook lies in the deep disappointment I felt toward her and my need to make sense of it. I often wondered if she loved my sister more than she loved me. Maybe I was the problem. I always felt distant from her. These doubts and emotional questions—*Am I lovable? Why doesn't she care for me the way I need her to?*—are things many readers can relate to. That's what gives the story its emotional weight. Over the course of writing that piece, I began to examine those feelings and try to answer a larger, more complicated question: *Why wasn't my mother maternal—and what did that have to do with me?* Many readers have grappled with disappointment in a parent or struggled to understand the emotional distance of someone they needed to love them.

The Importance of Pacing for an Emotional Journey

Once you've established the emotional hook—what truly matters to the character—you need to let the emotional journey unfold slowly and deliberately. That gradual unfolding is what makes an emotional arc engaging and satisfying. It builds tension, deepens understanding, and ultimately reaches a moment of emotional clarity or transformation. And no, this doesn't mean the story has to resolve in a happy way. Emotional resolution doesn't require joy—it requires *truth*. Sometimes, the most powerful emotional journeys end in heartbreak, disillusionment, or acceptance. What matters is that the emotional tension is explored and given space to evolve.

To make emotional moments land with impact, you need to craft the full arc of feeling—from its earliest stirrings to its final emotional note. If a character is about to experience a devastating loss, for example, the reader needs to understand what that loss means to them *before* it happens. The heartbreak doesn't come from the event itself—it comes from the contrast between what was and what's been lost. Show the reader all the things that make this loss so devastating—before it occurs.

When the emotional climax finally arrives, resist the urge to rush it. Let it unfold in real time. Slow down and allow the reader to feel each emotional beat as it happens. Use sensory detail, small physical gestures, and interior silence to convey the weight of the moment.

Emotional truth doesn't always come in the form of dramatic speeches or outbursts. Sometimes it shows up in silence, hesitation, or subtle reactions—a pause before speaking, a glance away, the way someone's fingers brush a photograph before setting it down. Pay attention to how people actually navigate their emotions in real life: some confront them head-on, while others deflect, retreat, or sit with them quietly. There are so many ways that emotions show themselves.

After the emotional high point of a story, resist the urge to cut immediately to the next plot event. Instead, give the moment space to settle. That doesn't mean dragging it out, but allowing a scene or two, or even just a few well-chosen paragraphs, where the character is reacting, reflecting, or reeling.

Let the emotion linger. Show how it lives in the body: a missed night of sleep, a hand trembling on a doorknob, the way someone flinches at a word or avoids a familiar object. Let it show in behavior: does the character withdraw, reach out, second-guess a decision? These small, honest reactions are where emotional realism lives. Emotion doesn't end with a climax; it ripples outward. Give the reader time to feel those ripples.

Before and After Example

BEFORE – Rushed and Abstract

Maya stormed out of the house, her heart pounding. She had finally said it. Finally told him how much he had hurt her.

The next morning, she packed her bags and left town.

What's missing:

- No time to process the emotional impact.
- No physical or behavioral cues showing how Maya is feeling.
- The reader is *told* something important happened but not invited to *feel* it.

AFTER – Emotionally Grounded and Specific

Maya stormed out of the house, her heart pounding. She had finally said it. Her hands were still shaking.

Outside, she leaned against the porch railing. The night air smelled like wood smoke and the roses her stepmother still tended. She pressed her palms to her eyes. She hadn't cried during the fight, but now that she was alone, the tears came.

The Compassionate Writer

She stayed out there for a long time. At one point, the porch light flicked on. Her father's shadow moved behind the front window. Then nothing.

Later, in the guest room, she lay awake. The words kept replaying: "You left me. You never came back." She thought she'd feel better after saying it. Instead, her chest felt hollow. She turned onto her side and drew her knees up to her chest.

In the morning, she didn't pack right away. She made coffee, sat at the kitchen table, and stared at the cracked sugar bowl between her hands.

Maybe he would come in. Maybe he wouldn't.

Either way, something had changed.

Why this version works:

- Sensory detail (wood smoke, roses, cracked sugar bowl) creates emotional atmosphere.
- Physical behavior (shaking hands, sleeplessness, curling up) shows the emotional aftermath.
- Pacing slows down the moment, letting it breathe.
- Emotional ripple is clear—we see how the confrontation affects her the next morning.

Things to Avoid

One of the biggest pitfalls in emotional writing is relying on clichés, which are overused expressions that feel generic. For example, a single tear rolling down the cheek, someone collapsing to their knees, or a passionate confession in the pouring rain. These tropes have been used so often that they have lost their impact.

Instead, focus on details unique to your character and their experience. If a character is heartbroken, what small, specific action might reveal their pain? Do they keep rereading an old text message? Do they set out two coffee mugs in the morning, forgetting they're now alone? In memoir, maybe you find yourself talking to someone who's no longer there, touching the clothes they'll never wear again, or reaching out to old friends who once knew them well—seeking connection through shared memory. These quiet, personal moments often carry more emotional truth than grand declarations. They stay with the reader because they feel real.

The Role of Conflict

As discussed in the previous chapter, conflict is the engine that moves a story forward. But it's the emotions surrounding conflict that shape an emotional journey. Conflict reveals what your characters want most and what it costs them to pursue their desires. When you tap into those deeper emotional stakes, conflict can force characters to confront the very things they've been trying to avoid—or it can reveal emotional truths they haven't yet acknowledged. That's what makes it such a powerful tool in crafting an emotional journey.

For example, imagine an argument between a parent and their adult child about career choices. On the surface, it may seem like a simple disagreement. But underneath, the parent might feel unappreciated after a lifetime of sacrifices, while the child feels suffocated by years of unmet expectations. The argument isn't really about careers—it's about love, identity, regret, and the need for recognition. Those are the emotional currents that give the scene its weight and complexity.

Conflict is essential to the emotional journey not just because it creates tension, but because it reveals hidden truths. It brings to the surface what characters might otherwise keep buried: their insecurities, disappointments, hopes, and vulnerabilities. Well-crafted conflict doesn't just push the plot forward—it pushes the character forward, often toward uncomfortable self-discovery or irreversible change.

What They Don't Say: The Power of Interiority

The most emotionally resonant stories don't just show what happens *to* a character—they show what happens *inside* them. This is interiority: the stream of thoughts, memories, questions, and observations that form the private soundtrack of your character's mind. These are the things they wouldn't say out loud—often because they're ashamed, afraid, or unwilling to admit what they truly think or feel. These moments show us what's really at stake.

Interiority is the emotional subtext brought to light. A character might say, "I'm so glad you're happily married," while privately thinking, *I wish he wasn't married to my sister. I wish he was my husband.* In memoir, interiority shows up when you write what you'd never say out loud—the thoughts you try to hide, even from yourself. These moments reveal vulnerability, contradiction, and emotional truth.

When we write interiority well, we don't just describe emotions—we create them in the reader. We let them step inside the character's inner world and feel what the character feels, even when the emotions are messy, contradictory, or hard to name. That's what makes a character feel fully alive. And that's what makes an emotional journey truly immersive.

Anne E. Beall, PhD

How to Write Interiority

- **Use a close-up point of view (POV).** First-person and deep third-person POV are the best tools for accessing interiority. In deep third, the narration is so aligned with the character's thoughts, perceptions, and emotions that it feels like we're inside their head. Example (deep third): *The room fell silent. Of course. They'd been talking about her. Sarah's stomach tightened. She should never have come.* Example (first person): *I entered the room, and it fell silent. I suddenly wondered if they had been talking about me. My stomach tightened, and I realized I never should have come.*
- **Let thoughts contradict actions.** A character smiling while thinking *I hope you choke on that toast* is more compelling than one who simply scowls. Complexity lives in contradiction.
- **Be specific.** Avoid abstract feelings like *"She was sad."* Instead, give us the exact thought: *I shouldn't miss him after what he did. But I do.*
- **Use sensory and physical cues.** Emotions live in the body—through a nervous twitch, sweaty palms, an aching stomach, or the rush of blood in one's ears. These physical cues can reveal what your character can't say out loud.
- **Don't resolve too soon.** Let your character sit in discomfort. Let them flinch from their own thoughts. This is where depth occurs. For example: *She shut the door and stood there, staring at the grain in the wood. It's done, she thought. But her hand was still on the knob. She told herself to walk away. Instead, she listened for footsteps on the other side. Nothing. Just the silence she'd come here to end.*

Ending with Emotional Honesty

Although stories don't need a happy ending, they do need an honest one. A satisfying ending doesn't tie up loose ends, but the resolution feels earned and true to the characters. For example, if a character has experienced loss, they may not "get over it" by the final page, but they may have found a way to carry their grief differently. If a character has been searching for love, they may not end up with a partner, but they may have discovered something valuable about themselves.

When shaping an ending for a work of fiction, ask yourself:

- What has my character learned or gained from this journey?
- What emotions do they carry forward?

When shaping the ending of a memoir, focus not just on what happened, but on what it *means*. Ask yourself the following questions:

- What have I come to understand about myself (or someone else) that I couldn't see then?
- What questions still linger—and what have I learned to live with?
- What emotional truths do I carry forward, even if the circumstances have changed?

Readers will feel satisfied when the ending feels real. When crafting an emotional ending, ask yourself: How do I want the reader to feel when they put this book down? What will linger with them?

Anne E. Beall, PhD

An Example of an Emotional Journey

The following is a fictional example of a clear emotional journey. The character experiences both highs and lows, and through these moments, undergoes meaningful transformation.

"A Cup of Tea"

It started with the tea.

Every morning, I make jasmine tea. It's my ritual—kettle on, mug in hand, quiet before the chaos of the day. But lately, it didn't taste right. Flat, somehow. I thought maybe the leaves were old. Or maybe I just needed more sleep.

Then the bruises showed up. Faint at first, like fingerprints on my thighs and arms. I didn't remember bumping into anything. I mentioned it during a check-up, offhand, like I wasn't worried. Because I wasn't. Not really.

The doctor ordered bloodwork. "Just in case," she said.

Two days later, she called.

"I'd like you to come in and talk about your results," she said gently. Something in her voice made my stomach turn cold.

In her office, I sat perfectly still as she said the word: leukemia. My brain refused to accept it. I smiled, nodded, took the pamphlets, heard her say things like "early stages," "treatment options," "we'll start soon."

I walked out in a daze. It didn't feel real.

At home, I boiled water and made tea again. It tasted like nothing.

I didn't tell my daughter Luna right away. She's only five. I didn't even say the word to my husband until that night, and even

The Compassionate Writer

then, I softened it. "They're still running tests," I told him. "It might not be serious."

But I knew. Deep down, I already knew.

The days blurred. People called. My sister cried. I answered every "How are you?" with "I'm fine." I wasn't. But I wasn't ready to say it out loud. Saying it made it real.

Then one afternoon, I watched Luna play on the living room floor, brushing her doll's hair with a tiny toothbrush. She gave the doll a name and made up a story about her. I felt something twist in my chest. What if I'm not here for this next year? What if I miss watching her grow?

That night, I sat in the dark and cried for the first time. Deep, full-body crying that made my ribs ache.

And then, I made a decision. I would fight.

Treatment began. Chemo. Hospitals. IVs. Nausea. My hair thinned and fell out in clumps. My skin turned pale. I barely recognized myself in the mirror.

One night, after a brutal session, I collapsed on the bathroom floor. My head spun. My fingers shook. I pressed my palm to the cold tile and whispered, "I can't do this."

I meant it.

Then I heard small footsteps.

Luna stood in the doorway in her pajamas, holding a drawing. A stick figure with a cape and a crown.

"It's you," she said. "You're my superhero."

I looked at her, this little person I made, and something in me—something fierce—came back to life. I kept going.

Weeks passed. Bloodwork. Good days. Bad days. Days I wanted to quit. Days I didn't.

And then one day, my doctor smiled and said, "Your numbers look excellent. You're in remission."

That night, I made jasmine tea.

It tasted like jasmine again.

Stage	Emotion	Story Moment
Beginning	Distracted, tired	"The tea didn't taste right. I thought I needed more sleep."
Diagnosis	Shock, disbelief	"She said the word: *leukemia*. My brain refused to accept it."
Denial	Numb, detached	"I answered every 'How are you?' with 'I'm fine.' I wasn't."
Realization	Grief, fear	"What if I'm not here for this next year?"
Decision to Fight	Determination	"And then, I made a decision. I would fight."
Low Point	Exhaustion, hopelessness	"I collapsed on the bathroom floor. 'I can't do this,' I whispered."
Turning Point	Hope, renewed strength	"Luna held a drawing. 'It's you,' she said. 'You're my superhero.'"
Resolution	Relief, quiet joy	"That night, I made jasmine tea. It tasted like jasmine again."

The Compassionate Writer

This example presents a clear emotional journey. It begins with the character feeling tired, followed by a shocking diagnosis that leads to numbness. As the reality sets in that she could die, grief takes hold. Then, a shift occurs. She becomes determined to fight the cancer. However, she later hits a low point, overwhelmed by exhaustion and hopelessness. It's during an interaction with her daughter that her hope is rekindled. She decides to keep fighting, and ultimately, she does—leading to feelings of relief and joy. This progression forms a compelling and coherent emotional arc, and the stark contrast between her lowest and highest points makes the journey feel authentic and hard-won.

Case Studies: How Great Writers Create Emotional Journeys

Ian McEwan's *Atonement* is a powerful example of how an author builds emotion over time. When thirteen-year-old Briony falsely accuses Robbie of assaulting her cousin, Cecilia, her misunderstanding doesn't just cause immediate damage. It shatters several lives, and the emotional fallout unfolds across decades. McEwan doesn't rush the consequences. Instead, he allows the emotional weight to accumulate slowly. Robbie is imprisoned and later sent to war; Cecilia becomes estranged from her family; and Briony gradually comes to understand the full extent of the harm she caused.

The novel's structure mirrors this emotional pacing. It moves from the sunlit innocence of the opening scenes, to the grim realism of wartime, to Briony's late-life reckoning. Each section deepens the emotional resonance. By the time we reach her final attempt at atonement—rewriting the past through fiction—the emotional devastation is undeniable, not because of one dramatic moment, but because of everything that came before it.

In *To Kill a Mockingbird* by Harper Lee, Scout Finch's emotional journey is one of growing awareness. At the beginning of the novel, she sees the world in terms of absolutes: right and wrong, good and bad. But as she witnesses injustice, cruelty, and the limitations of her own understanding, her perspective shifts. The moment she finally stands on Boo Radley's porch and sees the world through his eyes is not just a plot resolution, it is the culmination of her emotional transformation. The reader feels the full impact of her journey because we've experienced each step of it alongside her.

Great emotional journeys in storytelling—whether fiction or nonfiction—are built through contrasts, realizations, and quiet moments. Writers create these journeys by letting emotions evolve naturally through small actions and the slow unraveling of understanding. These journeys can leave a lasting impact, changing how we see the world long after the book is closed.

Below are some exercises to help you create an emotional journey in your own writing.

Exercise: Writing the Unspoken

Choose a moment in your story. Write it from deep inside your character's (or your own) perspective, using first-person or deep third-person POV. Describe what's happening internally. Include:

- Sensory detail: What does the character notice? What physical sensations arise in their body?
- Specific thoughts: What exact thoughts run through their mind? Let them be fragmented, contradictory, or uncomfortable.

- Contradiction: Show where their thoughts don't match their actions or words.
- Emotional discomfort: Don't resolve the feeling. Let it remain unresolved, complex, or messy.

Tip: Choose a quiet or subtle moment, not a dramatic one—this helps you focus on internal complexity rather than external action.

Exercise: Writing Emotion with Small Details

Think about a powerful emotional moment from your own life—a time when you felt deep joy, grief, love, or fear.

Now, write about that moment without directly naming the emotion. Instead, focus on sensory details and physical actions that reveal the feeling. What did you see, hear, or touch? How did your body react? Did your hands shake, your breath hitch, your heart race?

For example, instead of writing, "I was devastated," you might write: "I traced the rim of her coffee cup with my fingertip, staring at the untouched sugar packet beside it. Outside, a dog barked, but I didn't turn to look. The chair across from me remained empty." By showing rather than telling, you allow readers to experience the emotion rather than simply reading about it.

Exercise: Mapping an Emotional Arc

Choose a character (or yourself, if writing memoir), and map out the emotional journey. Follow these steps:

- **Define the Starting Emotion**: What does the character feel at the beginning? (Hopeful? Angry? Indifferent?) What are

the reasons for this feeling? What circumstances or beliefs shape this initial emotion?
- **Identify the Turning Points**: List three to five key moments that shift their emotions. What events, realizations, or interactions cause these changes? Are the shifts gradual or sudden?
- **Use Contrast**: Where can you introduce an emotional contrast to heighten the impact? Can a moment of hope make an eventual loss more painful? Can a struggle make a victory more meaningful?
- **Show the Final Emotion**: By the end, how has the character changed emotionally? What do they understand now that they didn't before? How does this change their actions or outlook?

Full Scene: Write a short scene that captures one of these emotional turning points. Focus on showing the shift—through small actions, dialogue, or sensory details—rather than simply stating the character's feelings.

Writing Prompts: Practice Creating an Emotional Journey

The First Stirrings of Emotion

- Write about a character who isn't yet aware of what they're feeling. Show how the emotion reveals itself through small actions or almost imperceptible body language before it reaches conscious awareness. Let the feeling grow—what causes it to surface?
- Write about the first stirrings of a deep hope or desire in your own life. What emotions began to rise? What future did you

start to imagine? Describe how that hope shaped your thoughts or actions over time and the emotions that occurred.

Emotional Pacing and Accumulation

- Describe a time when you felt mildly irritated, and the feeling slowly built into full-blown rage. Use small details, silences, or subtle triggers to show how the pressure grew until the emotion finally broke through.
- Write a romantic scene where the confession of love never comes. Build tension through silence, touch, or pauses. Let the yearning exist without resolution.

Turning Points

- Write a scene where you or a character breaks down in response to something small—a broken dish, a missed call, or a forgotten birthday. Let the moment reveal what's been building underneath.

Interiority and Emotional Contrast

- Write a scene in which you or a character says or does one thing but feels something completely different. Show the internal thoughts that this person would never utter aloud.
- Show two different time periods in your life or in a character's life to create emotional contrast. For example, depict early romance and then post-breakup; or a joyful moment with a parent, then that same person later in decline.

Emotional Conflict

- Write a scene of emotional conflict where both sides want something meaningful—but neither can say it directly. Show what underlies each person's perspective and why neither is "right." For example, both parents could disagree about where to send their child to school, a couple can disagree about money, etc.

Emotional Aftermath and Lingering Feelings

- Write about yourself or a character waking up the day after a major emotional event—loss, confession, breakthrough. How does the world feel now? What has changed internally? What small actions reveal these feelings?

Emotional Honesty and Catharsis

- Consider your main character at the end of your story. How do they live differently now as a result of everything they've been through? It doesn't have to be a happy ending—but it should feel emotionally honest. What truth would be most realistic?

Guided Visualization: Entering the World of Emotion

This guided visualization is designed to help you explore a moment of intense emotion—either your own or that of a character you've created. You'll be invited to step into that emotional world, feel it fully, and trace the journey it takes.

You may choose to read this slowly to yourself, record it and listen back, or simply close your eyes and move through the process in your mind. If strong emotions arise, breathe gently. You are in control at all times, and you can pause or stop whenever you need.

Begin by finding a quiet place where you won't be disturbed. Sit in a way that feels both grounded and comfortable—feet on the floor or tucked beneath you, spine tall but soft, shoulders relaxed.

The Compassionate Writer

Let your hands rest in your lap or wherever feels most natural. Take a slow, steady breath in… and exhale gently. Again, breathe in deeply—filling your lungs—and release. With each breath, allow yourself to sink a little deeper into stillness. Let your muscles soften. Let your thoughts settle. There is nowhere else you need to be. Just here.

Now, imagine that you are standing at the edge of an emotional world. This might be a moment from your own life, or from a character's life. Either way, it is a moment of intense feeling—perhaps tremendous joy, anger, heartbreak, grief, shame, fear, longing, or confusion.

You don't need to search too hard. Simply notice what emotion rises naturally. Let yourself be gently pulled toward a specific moment—when that feeling was strongest.

Before stepping fully into it, take in the setting. Where are you? Indoors or outside? What do you notice about the space? Who is there with you, if anyone? What time of day is it? What do you see, hear, or smell? Let the scene take shape slowly, like a dream coming into focus. There is no rush.

Now, when you're ready, step into the body of the person at the center of this scene. Whether it's you or a character you've created, step fully into their perspective.

You are no longer watching from the outside. You are this person now, standing in this emotional moment. Breathe into that.

Now consider: *How did I get here?* Begin to trace the path that led to this moment. What events unfolded? Recall the key moments along the way—specific conversations, decisions, actions, or turning points.

What did you want before this moment? What were you hoping for or expecting? What deeper need was driving you—love, safety, belonging, justice, approval?

Allow earlier memories to surface. Let them rise naturally, without forcing them. Move gently through these moments, pausing where something feels significant—especially anything connected to this emotional event. Linger there. Feel the texture of those memories—the sounds, sensations, and emotions they carry. Take your time. Let yourself fully explore anything that feels meaningful or revealing.

Follow the emotional thread forward to the moment when the feeling was most intense. Let yourself arrive there fully.

You are here now.

Take a breath.

Now ask yourself: What am I feeling in my body? Do you notice a tightness in your chest? A heaviness in your stomach? Are your hands cold? Are your shoulders tense? Do you feel flushed, frozen, shaky, or numb? What's happening behind your eyes? In your throat? In your jaw? Scan your body gently—without judgment—and notice what arises.

Now consider, What am I doing in this moment—and what do I wish I could do? Are you speaking? Silent? Crying? Yelling? Leaving? Laughing? Trying to hold it all together?

Stay with this. This is the center of the experience.

What thoughts are swirling through your mind? What words are you afraid to say aloud? What have you kept hidden—even from yourself?

Let the feelings come. Name them as they arise: shame, anger, fear, longing, betrayal, grief, relief, hope. Each one is welcome. Each one is part of the truth.

Now ask yourself: What happened next? Let the scene begin to move forward in time. Trace how the emotion began to shift. Maybe something softened—not right away, but eventually. Maybe something cracked open or fell away. Maybe something changed in how you saw yourself—or someone else.

Follow the emotional journey forward.

What lingered? What faded? What remained unresolved? How did the intensity evolve over time?

Keep moving forward until the feeling no longer holds the same charge. It may still be present—or it may be gone.

Pause here, in this quieter space. Ask yourself: What did I learn about this emotional journey?

Let whatever insights arise come naturally. There are no right answers—only your truth.

Take a breath to honor what you've seen and felt.

When you're ready, gently return to the present moment. You have journeyed through something meaningful.

Now, take time to write about this experience—and the threads that tie an emotional journey together.

*

Writing emotional journeys can stir up intense feelings—not just for your readers, but for you as the writer. Revisiting painful memories or confronting difficult truths on the page requires courage and care. In the next chapter, we'll explore how to write about sensitive subjects with honesty, respect, and emotional integrity—both for your audience and for yourself.

Chapter 9: Avoiding Exploitative or Harmful Narratives

"Writers, like all artists, must be careful not only with what they include in their stories but also with what they leave out. Silence can be just as powerful as words." — Haruki Murakami

Let's face it: the world is a minefield, and it's easy to be insensitive without intending to be. As writers, we engage with complex topics—relationships, identities, trauma, and societal challenges. But writing about them requires thoughtfulness and care. It's possible for a story to harm both the people it portrays and the readers it hopes to reach.

This chapter is about navigating difficult or sensitive topics in your writing with integrity and kindness—toward yourself, your characters (real or fictional), and your readers.

What is Exploitative Writing?

Exploitation in writing happens when a story presents painful, traumatic, or controversial events solely for shock value or entertainment. It's a narrative that doesn't examine the emotional depth of the experience or the potential harm it might cause people who have experienced something similar.

But that doesn't mean you should avoid difficult topics. In fact, many of the most powerful stories come from engaging with painful truths. The key is to handle those truths with intention, empathy, and awareness of your impact.

Let's say you're writing about a teenage girl named Amina who is humiliated when a private photo of her is shared without her

The Compassionate Writer

consent. The story explores themes of shame, betrayal, and the struggle to reclaim identity after a deeply personal violation. Here's how this narrative could be written exploitatively versus compassionately.

In an *exploitative version*, the moment her photo is leaked becomes a spectacle. The image is described in detail, and the reactions of others are portrayed through laughing, whispering, and pointing. Amina is reduced to a passive figure who is merely a backdrop to other characters' outrage or moral growth. Her inner world is ignored, and the narrative quickly shifts to how the school responds or how a friend intervenes and is cast as the hero.

In a *compassionate version*, the writer stays close to Amina's interior world. The scene might follow her through the hallway as she notices who meets her eyes and who looks away. She might wonder if she'll ever feel safe at school again, or she may replay the moment she chose to trust someone with the photo and blame herself for what's occurred. Rather than centering spectacle or resolution, the story focuses on Amina's agency—her silence, her rage, her decisions, even her uncertainty. The trauma is still present, but it's handled with emotional honesty, restraint, and respect for the complexity of her experience.

Unfortunately, this kind of exploitation is common in stories that portray violence against women. A frequent example is a narrative that opens with a graphic, detailed scene of sexual assault, only for the victim to vanish from the story entirely. The event serves only to justify a male character's revenge arc, rather than offering a meaningful exploration of the survivor's trauma, recovery, or agency.

The issue here isn't the inclusion of sexual assault—difficult subjects absolutely have a place in stories. There's nothing inherently wrong with depicting sexual violence, even in vivid terms, but writers must carefully consider the purpose behind including such scenes and what they intend to convey. Is the goal to portray the emotional toll of the experience with honesty and care? Or to explore how someone copes, survives, or begins to heal? When handled with depth and intention, these narratives can foster understanding. When used merely for shock value or plot advancement, they risk becoming exploitative.

Now imagine that a story about sexual assault is told from a different angle: a woman rebuilding her life afterward. The event is referenced only briefly, in restrained language, but her healing process—through friendships, boundaries, trust, and moments of vulnerability—is portrayed in detail. The focus is on her agency and growth, not her suffering alone. This kind of narrative honors the person at the center of the trauma, instead of using them as a means to drive someone else's story forward.

When you write with compassion, it protects the humanity of your characters, and it respects your readers' experiences. When you approach difficult subjects with empathy, you don't reduce people to symbols or plot devices, you show them as real, complex human beings. If you're writing about someone experiencing homelessness, for example, compassion means showing their hopes, fears, and dreams—not just their struggles. It also means recognizing that some readers will have lived through similar experiences, so you need to use language and imagery that respects their experience and isn't dismissive. Compassion will help you tell deeper, more honest

The Compassionate Writer

stories and it helps ensure that your work builds understanding instead of reinforcing stereotypes.

How Cognitive Shortcuts Shape Our Writing

Our brains are wired to take mental shortcuts. Psychologists call these *heuristics*—strategies that help us process complex information quickly by simplifying it. They're efficient, but not always accurate. When it comes to people, one of the most common heuristics we use is the stereotype.

As Macrae and colleagues discovered, stereotypes act as *"energy-saving devices."* They allow us to make rapid judgments with minimal mental effort by categorizing people based on traits like race, gender, age, or class. This may help us navigate the world quickly, but it becomes a serious liability in storytelling. When writers rely on stereotypes—whether consciously or not—they reduce characters to shallow labels rather than portraying them as fully human.

Another set of shortcuts that shapes our writing is *ingroup and outgroup bias*. Social psychologists Henri Tajfel and John Turner found that people naturally favor members of their own group—whether defined by race, gender, culture, or beliefs—and tend to view outsiders more negatively. We extend more empathy to people we see as "like us," and we're quicker to excuse their flaws or understand their pain. Conversely, we may unconsciously view those in the "outgroup" as threatening, one-dimensional, or even less deserving of compassion.

Even when our intentions are good, these cognitive patterns can lead us to write characters simplistically—especially those who are different from us. That's why it's often easier to explore the emotional complexity of someone who shares your background, and harder to give depth to someone you perceive as "other." But this is exactly where the most powerful, humane writing begins: by resisting simplification and writing against our natural biases.

How to Write About Sensitive Topics with Compassion

Conduct Extensive Research

If you're writing about experiences or identities outside of your own, conduct research. Read books, articles, and personal accounts, and interview people with this experience or identity. This will ensure you gain a deeper understanding of the humanity behind the topic.

Tips for Researching:

- Seek out voices from the community or experience you're writing about, especially those that reflect a range of perspectives.
- Avoid relying solely on secondhand accounts or academic sources if firsthand narratives are available.
- Ask yourself: "Am I representing this story with the nuance and care it deserves?"
- Ask yourself: "Is this a story for *me* to tell?"

Avoid Stereotypes and Simplifications

Stereotypes flatten characters into a single dimension, reducing their humanity. Compassionate writing digs deeper, exploring the full range of experiences, emotions, and motivations that make each character unique. For example:

The Compassionate Writer

- A villain shouldn't be evil for the sake of being evil. Try to show the fears, wounds, or beliefs that drive their actions.
- A marginalized character shouldn't exist solely to teach the protagonist a lesson. Give them their own goals and a rich inner life.

A few years ago, I took a writing class where we were assigned to write from the perspective of someone we didn't know well. I chose to step into the shoes of a Nigerian internet scammer. At the time, I had only seen them as villains, and I had made no effort to understand their circumstances.

To write the story, I researched who is typically behind these scams and how they operate. I learned that many of these individuals have limited economic opportunities and live in difficult conditions. For some, scamming is one of the few ways for them to make a living.

After finishing the story, I decided to take it a step further. I engaged with several internet scammers online and shared my work with them. While most were only interested in reading it for money, a few agreed to do so for free. It was enormously gratifying when those individuals told me I had captured their experience accurately.

This experience changed how I think about stereotypes in storytelling. Here's a clear example of how a character can either reinforce a harmful trope or resist it:

- **Exploitative**: In a crime thriller, a gang member from a Latinx community is described only through clichés—tattoos, violence, and drug use. He has no name, no backstory, and no dialogue beyond threats. He exists solely

to create danger. This kind of writing dehumanizes the character, and it's not very creative. There's no complexity in the character, and no reason for the reader to care about this person.
- **Compassionate**: In a more thoughtful version of the same story, the gang member still poses a threat—but he also has a name, a past, and an interior world. Maybe he's just out of juvenile detention and struggling to stay clean while caring for his younger brother. His tattoos still mean something, but the story gives us glimpses of why he chose them—what they covered up, or what they tried to prove. He still makes dangerous choices, but we see the fear behind them, the loyalty that drives him, and the small moments of hesitation that suggest he might want something else. The tension remains, but now the character is a person, not a trope.

Focus on the Emotional Truth, Not the Shock Value

Difficult topics often come with intense imagery, but writing with compassion means focusing on the emotional impact rather than the graphic details. For example:

- **Exploitative**: The novel dwells on gruesome battlefield violence with blow-by-blow detail—limbs torn off, blood spraying, bodies piled high—but the characters themselves remain emotionally flat. There's no reflection, no emotional processing, and no sense of how the violence affects them beyond surviving the moment. The scenes exist primarily to shock or entertain.
- **Compassionate**: The same novel still includes combat scenes, but the focus is on how the characters experience the

violence—what they think in the moment, how they dissociate or freeze, how the fear or guilt registers in their bodies. Later, a veteran flinches at the pop of a grocery bag or avoids sitting with his back to the door in a restaurant. The trauma is revealed not just through spectacle, but through subtle, human moments that show how violence stays with him long after the war.

If you're writing about a violent event, ask yourself:

- What emotions are the characters experiencing?
- How is this moment shaping their relationships, worldview, or their inner life?
- What's the larger significance of this event within the story?

By focusing on the emotional truth, you invite readers to connect with the humanity of the situation rather than being overwhelmed by the event.

Consider Your Own Emotional Limits

Writing about sensitive or traumatic experiences, especially those drawn from your own life, can be emotionally draining. That's why it's essential to extend the same compassion toward yourself that you offer to your readers and characters.

Even when telling your own story, it's possible to slip into exploitative patterns: oversharing painful details without context, reliving trauma without reflection, or focusing so narrowly on the pain that the deeper meaning is lost. Give yourself space to process and write with care—not just for others, but for your own well-being. Here are two contrasting examples:

- **Exploitative:** A memoirist includes every painful detail of an abusive experience, feeling obligated to "go there" for the sake of honesty. But in doing so, they retraumatize themselves, writing from a place of emotional harm rather than reflection.
- **Compassionate**: Another writer chooses to tell their story through metaphor and emotional nuance, focusing on the journey through grief, resilience, and self-forgiveness. They leave out graphic details, trusting that their truth will still be felt, and that protecting their own well-being is part of the writing process.

Tips for Protecting Your Emotional Well-Being:

Here are some tips for protecting yourself as you write. Take breaks. Writing about difficult topics doesn't have to happen all at once. Set clear boundaries around how much of your story you're ready to share—and give yourself permission to leave some parts out.

If your writing stirs up unresolved emotions, seek support from trusted friends or a therapist. Sometimes, it helps to process the experience with a professional before putting it on the page. Give yourself time. Understanding what happened, how it affected you, and what it means now is not always immediate. Be patient with your own growth.

Think About the Reader's Experience

As you write, consider how your words might affect readers—especially those who have lived through the experiences you're depicting. Although you can't predict how every reader will respond, you can approach writing with empathy. A thoughtful

The Compassionate Writer

narrative can affirm and empower, whereas a careless one can alienate or cause harm.

Here are two examples that illustrate the difference:

- **Exploitative**: A novel follows a woman struggling with opioid addiction. Although the story includes scenes from her past, its emphasis is on her decline—repeated relapses, lost relationships, and an overdose that ends the book. The narrative tone suggests she had multiple chances to change but didn't. Readers are left with a sense of tragedy, but little of the woman's inner complexity, agency, or the broader context of her struggle. For some, especially those with lived experience, the story may feel as if it reinforces stigma and stereotypes rather than offering understanding.

- **Compassionate**: In another version of the same story, the woman also relapses—but the narrative centers her humanity throughout. Her choices are rooted in past trauma, but also in love, loyalty, and fear. Even when she makes mistakes, we understand why. After her overdose, the story doesn't end, it deepens. We see her choose treatment, repair a relationship, or simply survive another day. The narrative doesn't offer false hope, but it resists flattening her into a symbol of failure. The story gives her dignity, depth, and the ongoing possibility of change.

Writing about difficult topics can be challenging. As you review your work, ask yourself:

- Have I approached this topic with care and integrity?
- Does my story offer some hope, healing, or insight alongside the difficult moments?

- Am I being honest without including unnecessary or gratuitous details?

Balancing Honesty and Compassion

Balancing honesty and compassion is essential in good writing. Compassion means recognizing another person's humanity and trying to understand their experience and to see the world through their eyes. In writing, compassion means telling the truth, even when it's messy or painful, in a way that honors the dignity of everyone involved. Honesty shows what happened. Compassion tells a deeper story.

If you're writing a memoir about a difficult parental relationship, honesty might mean acknowledging the ways your parents failed you. Compassion invites you to also explore the context—what pressures or traumas might have shaped their behaviors? It doesn't excuse harm, but it allows you to write with understanding rather than judgment.

The same is true in fiction. Compassion encourages you to create fully developed characters and to explore what drives them. Even if a character's actions are destructive, writing with empathy helps you show them as human—flawed, complicated, and sometimes a reflection of the reader.

Sensitivity Readers

A good way to avoid writing something harmful or exploitative is to seek out sensitivity readers—people who share the identity or lived experience you're portraying. They can review your work to flag any harmful stereotypes or inaccuracies. They can help you navigate complex topics with greater accuracy. Even well-intentioned writers can unconsciously reinforce damaging tropes, and sensitivity readers help ensure that portrayals are respectful, thoughtful, and nuanced. Their feedback can also add depth and authenticity to your story by highlighting details or perspectives you might not have considered. Using a sensitivity reader is especially important when you're writing about a race, ethnicity, culture, or experience that isn't your own.

You can often find sensitivity readers through writing groups, social media, or professional networks. To get the most out of the process, approach their feedback with an open mind, especially if it challenges your original assumptions. Remember that the goal isn't to defend your story, it's to make it stronger and more honest. And it's important to know that sensitivity readers are not censors; they offer insight and guidance, but you, as the writer, need to make the final creative choices.

Sensitivity readers aren't a substitute for thorough research, but they offer essential insights that can elevate your story. If your work involves marginalized identities or vulnerable topics, a sensitivity reader can help ensure your characters feel authentic—and that your portrayal supports, rather than harms, the communities being represented.

Still, the responsibility begins with you. As a writer, it's important to build your own awareness and intention. The following exercises are designed to help you write in a way that is compassionate, not exploitative.

Exercise: Break the Stereotype

Choose a character or group in your story that could easily fall into a stereotype. Write a scene that challenges this stereotype by showing the depth of them as a person or revealing an unexpected side of them. For example, a stoic warrior might reveal a love for poetry, or a villain might struggle with self-doubt.

Exercise: Writing with Compassion and Responsibility

Step 1: Choose a Difficult Topic in Your Story

Identify a sensitive or challenging subject you're writing about (e.g., trauma, injustice, mental health, abuse, or loss).

Step 2: Write a Scene that Centers Humanity

Write a scene that brings this topic to life by focusing on the humanity of the people involved. Let their emotions, hopes, fears, and complexities come through. Stay away from sensationalism or graphic details. Instead, show the emotional impact through small moments—what they notice, how they react, what they long for or struggle with. Subtle, honest details will speak volumes.

Step 3: Reflect on Your Choices

After writing, reflect on the scene:

- Did I write with empathy for all the characters involved?
- Did I avoid stereotypes or oversimplifications?
- How might this scene resonate with readers who've experienced something similar?

If something feels off, revise with compassion in mind.

The Compassionate Writer

Writing Prompts

The following prompts are designed to help you apply the ideas from this chapter.

Challenging Stereotypes and Surface Narratives

- Write a scene in which a character makes a well-intentioned but ignorant assumption about another person's culture, gender, body, or background. Show the discomfort and tension that follows—not through lecturing, but through the emotional fallout of the moment.
- Write a scene where a privileged character offers charity or advice to a marginalized character—and faces unexpected resistance. Explore how both characters experience the interaction differently.
- Create a character who is usually vilified in mainstream media—perhaps a gang member, a teen mom, or someone addicted to drugs—and show a moment where they are tender, wise, or deeply human.

Centering Humanity Without Exploiting Pain

- Write a scene in which a character reflects on a painful memory, but instead of describing what happened, show how it affects their present—what they avoid, what they say or don't say, what triggers unexpected emotion. <u>Do not</u> describe the trauma that happened.
- Depict a character experiencing mental illness, but resist making it melodramatic. Focus on the mundane ways the experience shapes their daily life—what they eat, how they sleep, what their interactions are like with others.

- Create a character who is grieving, but focus on the small, almost invisible ways it shows up—how they get dressed, how they speak, how they react to small frustrations.

Writing with Ethical Awareness and Reflection

- Identify specific areas where you'd like a sensitivity reader to focus their feedback. Consider the character's identity, background, and lived experiences, as well as any scenes or moments that might raise concerns. Make a list of the input you're seeking and be clear about what you're unsure of— whether it's the risk of reinforcing a stereotype, missing cultural nuance, or unintentionally causing harm.
- Reflect on a character you are writing or have written. Ask: *What are the risks of how I'm portraying this character? What blind spots might I have?* Write a paragraph honestly answering these questions.

Honoring Complexity and Reclaiming Power

- Imagine a marginalized character reading a popular book or watching a film that misrepresents them. Write their internal monologue as they react—what frustrates them? What would they change? What do they wish people understood?
- Write a scene in which a marginalized character tells their own story—without interruption, correction, or outside narration. Let them control the tone, the pacing, and what details they choose to share or withhold. What do they emphasize? What do they leave out?

The Compassionate Writer

Guided Visualization: The Ripple Effect of Your Story

Find a quiet, comfortable space. Let your body relax. Take a deep breath in... and out. Again, inhale deeply, letting the air expand within you... and exhale slowly, releasing any tension from your shoulders, your jaw, your hands. Let yourself soften. Allow your mind to settle.

Now, imagine yourself standing on a small island in the center of a still, circular lake. Across the way is a sandy shore, which encircles this quiet lake. The air is quiet. The only sound is your own breath. The surface of the water is smooth as glass, reflecting the sky above.

You look down at your hand. You are holding a single stone. This stone is your story. It carries everything you have written, imagined, and shaped—the characters, the emotions, the truths. When you are ready, breathe in... and toss it into the lake.

Watch as it falls, cutting through the still surface. Ripples spread outward, one after another. Your story has left you. It is moving outward into the world. Who will it reach first?

Now, see people appear at the water's edge along the sandy shore. Some are readers you know—friends, family, and fellow writers. Others are strangers you have never met, people whose lives will be touched by your story in ways you cannot predict.

One person kneels beside the water, watching the ripple reach them. Imagine they are someone who shares the experience you have written about.

As the ripple touches them, watch their reaction: Do they feel seen? Heard? Understood? Do they feel hurt? Misrepresented? Reduced to a stereotype? Do they find comfort in your story—or does it open an old wound?

Observe. Do not justify. Do not explain. Simply watch.

They look up at you. What do they say? Do they thank you for telling a truth that needs to be told? Or do they ask you to reconsider how you wrote their experience?

Listen. Stay present. Let them finish.

Now, ask them: "What do you need from my story?"

Wait. Let their answer come, even if it surprises you.

As you step back, you watch the ripples continue outward, reaching more people. Others step forward from the edges of the water. Each one, touched by the ripple of your words, has a response. What do they tell you? Listen to them closely. Listen without defending, without explaining. Simply receive what they offer you.

When all have stepped forward, take a deep, steady breath. With what you have learned, ask yourself what you will rewrite, what you will do more research on, and what you will add to your story.

Breathe in… and out. Slowly, the water fades. The ripples quiet. The world around you returns to stillness. You feel the ground beneath you. You are back.

Take a few moments to write. Let the words flow freely. There is no right answer—only deeper understanding. Your words have power. Use them well.

*

As writers, we care deeply about the impact our words have. But writing isn't just a responsibility; it can also be a form of care. In the next chapter, I'll explore how writing can be a tool for healing for both the writer and the reader.

Chapter 10: Writing to Heal: How Compassion Transforms Both Writer and Reader

"One writes not to be read but to breathe… one writes to survive."
— Anne Morrow Lindbergh

Writing has long been recognized as a powerful tool for healing. When we put our thoughts and emotions into words, we begin to understand ourselves and the world around us more clearly. As Joan Didion famously said, "I don't know what I think until I write it down." Writing allows us to process grief, untangle confusion, and release emotions we've been carrying, sometimes without even realizing it. Psychologist James Pennebaker, whose research explores the therapeutic effects of writing, notes that "Writing down a past trauma, stressful or emotional experience can improve both your physical and emotional health." Julia Cameron puts it simply: "Writing is medicine." Through writing, we don't erase the pain—we move through it, and sometimes beyond it.

But writing doesn't only heal the writer. It can also be a source of healing for others. When we share our struggles and reflections, we give readers permission to explore their own truths. Whether through memoir or fiction, the stories we tell have the power to reach beyond us, offering comfort and insight to others, especially those who may be going through something similar now or in the future.

I've experienced this firsthand. I wrote a piece titled *Glimpses* about my estrangement from my daughter and son. Putting that experience into words, and trying to make sense of it, has been profoundly healing. The pain hasn't disappeared, but it no longer cuts as deeply. Through writing, I've begun to understand something that once felt incomprehensible. What has deepened that healing is the response from others. Many readers have reached out to say the piece helped them make sense of their own estrangement—and reminded them they're not alone.

In this chapter, I'll explore how writing with compassion can become a path to healing for yourself and for your readers.

How Writing Heals the Writer

Writing is, at its core, an act of reflection. It isn't just about recounting events or crafting narratives—it's a way of understanding one's inner world. This can be transformative, helping you in three ways:

Understanding Your Emotions

Emotions can feel overwhelming. However, as you put feelings into words, you may begin to see what they're telling you, or where they come from. Writing turns raw emotion into something you can look at, understand, and learn from.

For example, writing about anger might reveal that beneath it lies deep disappointment in someone, or the feeling that you are not valued. It may trace back to an earlier experience, repeating patterns you've carried for years. You might also discover that anger contains shades of sadness or fear. Exploring joy, on the other hand, could uncover a sense of hope you hadn't fully recognized. Writing can show the expectations you carry and offer insight into the stories that shape your emotions. It can become a safe and productive space to engage with your emotions, gently turning confusion into understanding.

The Compassionate Writer

Reframing Your Experiences

Psychologists and narrative therapists have long observed that writing can help people reframe painful experiences through the lens of growth and self-compassion. When we carry pain or trauma, it's easy to get stuck in narratives of victimhood, regret, or blame. Writing allows us to revisit and reshape those experiences. As Brené Brown writes, "When we deny our stories, they define us. When we own our stories, we get to write the ending." While we can't change what happened, writing can help us change how we live with it.

For example, writing about a romantic breakup might help you realize how the experience taught you about your boundaries or desires. Writing about a failure might reveal the resilience you built afterward. Storytelling allows us to reshape the meaning of the past, not by rewriting events, but by discovering the deeper truths they hold for ourselves.

Releasing What No Longer Serves You

Sometimes, writing something down can help to release it from your mind or heart. When you write about difficult experiences with honesty and compassion, you create space to let go of what you've been carrying. Whether it's anger, guilt, or unresolved grief, writing can help you process your emotions and move forward.

In their book *Opening Up by Writing It Down*, psychologists James Pennebaker and Joshua Smyth describe numerous studies showing that expressive writing—putting difficult emotions into words—can improve mental health, reduce stress, and even strengthen the immune system. In one study, participants who wrote for just fifteen minutes a day over several days about traumatic experiences reported lower anxiety and greater overall well-being. As award-winning author Nikki Grimes said, "The urge to write can be a powerful force that helps us face and survive difficult experiences." Writing, therefore, isn't only a creative outlet—it can also be a powerful form of self-care.

Answering a Major Question to Assist with Healing

One of the most powerful ways writing can support healing is by helping to explore central questions—ones that linger beneath the pain. After a traumatic or deeply emotional experience, we often find ourselves circling the same thoughts, trying to understand what happened. Writing offers a space to face that question directly with compassion.

This question is often the one that may haunt you when you speak about what you've been through. It might be:

- Why did this happen to me?
- Am I to blame for this?
- How did I not see this coming?
- How do I move forward after this?
- How do I make sure this never happens again?
- How do I forgive—myself, or someone else?

When you find your central question, it can shape your writing—guiding how you explore the experience, what moments you focus on, and how you eventually bring the reader into your journey. It can help others who may be struggling with the same experience and who are asking themselves the same question.

I know what it's like to wrestle with the need to understand a painful experience. For years, I asked myself why I was estranged from my children—and what I had done wrong. Turning that question over in my writing helped me process my grief and see the

The Compassionate Writer

situation's complexity more clearly. In working through it on the page, I learned to extend compassion not only to myself but also to them. Over time, I realized that sharing this exploration might also offer guidance to others facing estrangement in their own lives.

How Writing Heals the Reader

Stories have the power to remind people they're not alone, to validate their emotions, and to offer hope. Writers explore a vast range of life experiences—grief, trauma, illness, betrayal, recovery—and the wide spectrum of feelings that come with them. I've read stories about death that held both sorrow and relief, stories of illness that included not just fear but anger, boredom, and moments of unexpected joy. These stories don't always present their characters as brave or noble—sometimes they show them as confused, ashamed, or emotionally numb. And that honesty is what makes them powerful. By reflecting our complexity back to us, stories can help readers feel seen, understood, and less alone in their own emotional journeys. Here are some ways that writing heals readers.

Stories Normalize Human Struggles

When you write honestly about your own struggles, you allow readers to see their own challenges as valid and normal. People who read your work will recognize themselves in your words and realize their emotions and experiences are simply part of being human.

For example, a memoir about living with anxiety or depression might bring comfort to someone who feels isolated by their own mental-health challenges. A novel about a grieving character might offer solace to a reader who is currently navigating a major loss.

Writing doesn't have to offer solutions. Sometimes simply naming the struggle is enough.

Stories Offer a Path to Healing

When you write about how you've faced and grown through difficult experiences, you provide readers the idea that healing is possible. Seeing that someone else has survived and managed their life after trauma can be profoundly inspiring to a reader in the midst of their own pain. Your words may encourage them to reflect, to seek help, or to see their lives in a new light. Even if your story doesn't end with a perfect resolution, showing that growth is possible can still offer hope.

Stories Connect Us

Writing can create a bridge between writer and reader. When you pour yourself onto the page, you invite others to step closer to your story. I have experienced this connection as both an author and a reader. At times, a piece has resonated so deeply with me that I've reached out to the author to say how much their words meant. It felt as if I knew them, as if they had become part of my inner world. One of those moments came when I read *Swimming with Maya* by Eleanor Vincent. Her daughter had died; mine was lost to estrangement. Though our circumstances were different, her honest portrayal of grief—its phases, its weight, its guilt—reflected my own experience in ways I hadn't fully named. I felt less alone. The book moved me so deeply that I wrote to her. That connection across distance and pain reminded me of the profound way stories unite us. And there have been countless occasions when readers have written to me. Even when no words are exchanged, a connection forms—a silent bond between two people through the power of story.

The Compassionate Writer

Practical Steps for Writing to Heal

Writing as a healing practice begins with kindness toward yourself. This means letting go of pressure to be eloquent and to have it all figured out. You don't need to write something profound. You only need to show up with honesty. Writing to heal isn't about crafting perfect sentences or resolving your pain on the page. It's about giving yourself space to explore what you feel, what you remember, and what still lingers. It's about allowing yourself to feel confused, raw, even angry—and meeting those parts of yourself without judgment. Healing begins not with answers, but with permission to feel your emotions, and to write through it, one word at a time.

Write About Emotional Truths

When writing to heal, what matters most isn't the precise accuracy of events but the truth of your emotions. Healing often comes not just from recounting what happened, but from allowing yourself to feel it, name it, and see it in a new light. Writing offers a space to ask: *What did this experience mean to me? How did it shape me? What am I still carrying from it now?*

You don't need to start with a timeline or a perfectly told story. Sometimes, you just need to begin—without knowing where the writing will take you. One helpful approach is to focus on a single emotional moment, rather than trying to explain everything at once. Choose one experience that still lingers in your memory and write your way into it.

You might ask yourself:

- What did it feel like inside my body?
- What were the thoughts that were swirling in my mind?

- What did I most want to happen in that moment?
- What did I fear, lose, or long for?

Emotional truth may not be easy to access, but writing is a way of gently bringing it forward. After you write, take a few moments to sit with what you uncovered. Ask yourself:

- What does this moment still want to teach me?
- What do I need to hear from myself right now?
- What part of me is asking for care or compassion?

Let these reflections guide your next steps—whether that's more writing, a time to reflect quietly, or simply a moment of tenderness toward yourself.

Be Honest, but Gentle

Writing to heal doesn't mean reliving every painful detail, exposing yourself to further trauma, or putting your safety at risk. You get to decide how much to share and how deeply to go. Strive for balance in your writing, giving yourself both honesty and care. Below are some tips to help you be kind to yourself when writing about something painful.

- Write for yourself first, without worrying about how it will be received. You can always decide later what to edit or omit.
- Take breaks when the material feels overwhelming. These can be breaks of a few minutes, a few hours, a few days, or many months. Sometimes it takes a while to confront things in our writing, and you need to be patient with yourself.
- If you're writing about trauma, consider working with a therapist alongside your writing practice.

The Compassionate Writer

Writing without Re-Traumatizing: The Doorway Method

When writing about traumatic experiences, it's important to move at your own pace. You don't need to relive the event in order to write about it. One way to approach difficult material is to imagine the memory as a room with a doorway.

You don't have to walk all the way in. You can stand in the doorway and write only what you can see from there—the physical details, the mood, the setting, the atmosphere. Stay at a distance that feels manageable. If it seems safe, you might move a little closer and explore more. But if it doesn't, you can always step back or close the door entirely.

This method helps you stay grounded and in control. It reminds you that you have choices in how you approach painful material. Writing can be a powerful tool for healing—but only when it respects the boundaries your body and mind are ready to hold.

The Reader's Journey

As you write with compassion for yourself, you can also think about how your story might resonate with someone else. Ask yourself:

- What emotions do I want readers to take away from this story?
- How can I offer them hope, insight, or connection?
- Are there places where I might overwhelm or alienate the reader?

It's amazing how simply writing about our experiences to help ourselves can also be healing for the reader. In her book *Big Magic*, Elizabeth Gilbert suggests that by trying to make sense of your own world, you often end up healing yourself—and others—without even intending to. As she explains:

> "I once wrote a book in order to save myself. I wrote a travel memoir in order to make sense of my journey and my own emotional confusion. All I was trying to do with that book was figure myself out. In the process, though, I wrote a story that apparently helped a lot of other people figure themselves out—that was never my intention."

That book was *Eat Pray Love*.

Examples of Writing to Heal

Cheryl Strayed, Tiny Beautiful Things

In her collection of advice columns, *Tiny Beautiful Things*, Cheryl Strayed writes with honesty and compassion, often drawing from her own life to help others make sense of theirs. She revisits her own grief, heartbreak, and mistakes with tremendous vulnerability. It's her willingness to tell the truth about her life that makes this book so deeply healing for those who read it.

One powerful example is her reflection on leaving her first marriage. Her husband was kind and loving, yet she felt a persistent urge to leave—something she couldn't explain at the time. Through writing, she came to see that this choice was both important and necessary to her journey. Many readers can relate to that feeling of being in the wrong relationship or situation without fully understanding why. By putting words to a complex, confusing experience, she not only found clarity for herself but also offered comfort and insight to others facing similar struggles.

The Compassionate Writer

Eleanor Vincent, Swimming with Maya

One book that has stayed with me is *Swimming with Maya* by Eleanor Vincent. In it, she recounts the devastating loss of her nineteen-year-old daughter, Maya, who died in a freak accident just after being accepted to UCLA. What makes this memoir so powerful is the honesty with which Eleanor portrays her emotional world. She blames herself, replays the past, and questions her choices as a mother, even while honoring the deep bond she shared with her daughter.

As the story unfolds, she begins to accept that sometimes accidents simply happen, though the search for meaning never ends. One of the most moving parts is her decision to donate Maya's organs—eventually meeting the man who received her daughter's heart. That connection becomes an unexpected thread of healing, a way for Maya's life to continue touching others.

Swimming with Maya is a stunning example of how writing through grief can create not only personal healing but also deep connection with others. Vincent's courage to ask hard questions—and lean into them—makes this book unforgettable.

I asked Eleanor if writing this book was healing, and she said:

> "I began writing the book weeks after Maya died. I wrote to survive, just as Anne Morrow Lindbergh says. To peel back layers of denial, I had to write slowly. I wrote to break my sense of unreality, the cognitive dissonance that overwhelmed me. The entire process took more than a decade. During those ten years, the nature of the healing changed. It morphed from survival to deeper understanding, and

finally to accommodation—but not full acceptance—of the truth that Maya was never coming back.

Hearing her heart beat in Fernando's chest and writing about the experience helped me hold a double vision: Although Maya was never coming back, she wasn't fully gone either because a vital part of her was keeping him alive.

As publication approached, the focus shifted entirely to the reader. I rewrote huge swaths of the manuscript. I wanted the story to be accessible and compelling. That focus on craft was healing in a different way. It made me realize how deeply I loved writing. I was more than a mother with a story of loss. I was a trained writer with deep dedication to vibrant storytelling. That commitment has carried me through three decades without Maya's physical presence."

Writing as a Source of Forgiveness

One of the most powerful ways writing can help us heal is by teaching us to forgive ourselves. We all have moments we look back on with regret—choices we wish we'd made differently, people we've hurt, actions we would undo if we could. These memories linger, shaping how we see ourselves. Writing offers a way to face them with honesty and compassion, and in doing so, begin to release their hold.

In her memoir *Again in a Heartbeat*, Susan Weidener writes about losing her husband to cancer and the many emotions she faced during their final years together. She shared in an interview that writing the book helped her come to terms with her own imperfections and to forgive herself for not being a better wife during his illness. Through writing, she was able to face the guilt she carried and to transform it.

She is not alone. Many writers discover that putting their experiences into words helps them soften the harsh judgments they've held against themselves. The page becomes a place where they can be honest, reflect, and eventually let go.

Writing also helps us to forgive others. That doesn't mean excusing hurtful behavior or pretending everything is fine. But it can mean we no longer carry the weight of someone else's actions. Through writing, whether through memoir, fiction, poetry, or even letters we never send, we can help to heal these deep wounds.

When we write with emotional honesty, something beautiful happens: readers see themselves in our stories. They recognize their own regrets, and some may even begin to forgive—both themselves and others. That's the power of writing. By finding the courage to forgive on the page, we not only heal ourselves but also offer healing to others.

Below are some exercises to help you use writing to heal.

Exercise: Discovering Your Big Question

Step 1: Freewrite about an Experience

Choose a significant emotional event that still lives within you—something you find difficult to think about. It might be something that happened to you, or something you did and now regret. Whatever the situation, let it be one that carries emotional weight.

Note: please approach difficult memories with care. If a memory is overwhelming, feel free to pause, step away, or just skip it entirely.

Set a timer for ten minutes and write freely. Don't worry about grammar, structure, or whether it makes sense—just let the words come. If you're unsure where to begin, these prompts might help:

- What happened?
- What feeling do I still experience about it?

Step 2: Find the Question That Haunts You

Look back over what you wrote and ask yourself:

- What do I most need to understand about this experience?
- What question underlies some of this writing?

Write down the one major question that stands out. This is the heart of your story.

Step 3: How Could Your Answer Help Others?

Now, reflect on your question and ask:

- If I had an answer to this, how could it help someone else?

Step 4: Structuring Your Story Around the Question

- Show the moment when this major question first arose, and how you've come to understand the answer over time. You can write a story that follows your journey to make sense of this mystery or uncover the truth behind it.
- Explore how the event unfolded chronologically—what led up to it, based on your answers to the earlier questions. You can write a story that traces all the experiences, choices, or patterns that brought you to that moment.

The Compassionate Writer

Exercise: The Letter You Need

Write a letter to yourself as if you were speaking to a dear friend. Address something you've been struggling with—grief, shame, self-doubt, or anything else—and offer yourself the same compassion you would offer someone you love.

Ask yourself:

- What do I need to hear right now?
- What would kindness toward myself look like in this situation?
- In what ways am I being hard on myself?
- What can I feel good about in this situation?

This exercise can help you access a deeper sense of self-compassion and clarity, which will enrich your writing.

Writing Prompts

The following prompts are designed to help you explore experiences that carry emotional weight—moments that can become a source of healing for yourself and others. These are not just storytelling exercises; they are invitations to reflect, to uncover deeper truths, and to assist in the work of healing. Again, some memories can be hard to revisit. If this feels like too much at any point, you should pause. Do what feels right for you.

Writing to Heal Yourself

- Write about something you've carried shame about—something you've kept hidden or judged yourself negatively for. What truth lies underneath the shame? What do you know now that you didn't know then?

- Write about the moment when pain became meaningful—when something difficult started to feel like part of your becoming. What changed in you? What was the spark that lit that shift?
- Tell the story of something or someone that saved you. It might have been a person, a book, a song, a belief, or even a stranger's small kindness. How did it arrive in your life, and what did it awaken?
- Describe a time when you surprised yourself with strength or clarity. What did you do that you didn't think you could? What did that moment reveal about your resilience?
- Write about an emotion you don't often give yourself space to feel—jealousy, rage, longing, tenderness. When did it show up? What did it want from you? What would it say if it had a voice?

Writing to Heal Others

These prompts are designed to help you write in a way that becomes a lifeline for someone else. Think of them as a way to turn your own experiences into a gift for someone else.
- Write a letter to someone you've never met but who is struggling with the same kind of pain you've known. What do you want them to know? What truth could you offer them?
- Choose a single sentence that helped you heal. Maybe it came from a book, a stranger, a therapist, or your own journal. Build a scene around that moment. Who said it? What did it change?

- Write about the impact of small kindnesses—a knowing glance, a casual check-in, someone using your name. Show how those quiet moments can be deeply healing.
- Imagine a reader picking up your story during their darkest hour. What do you want them to feel by the end? Write that closing passage now—something that holds space for their pain and offers the faintest light.
- Write about a moment when you forgave someone—or when someone forgave you. What led up to that moment, and how did it feel? What shifted as a result, and how does it feel now, looking back? What did you learn from this experience?

Guided Visualization: The Mountain of Wisdom

This visualization is designed to help you use writing as a path to healing—both for yourself and for others who need your story. It's a guided journey up a mountain, where you'll meet a wise Sage, connect with your inner wisdom, and remember why your voice matters.

You can read this slowly and let your imagination guide you. You might also choose to record yourself reading it aloud and listen to it later with your eyes closed. Or you can bring the core ideas and imagery of this visualization onto the mat if you have a current meditation practice.

Take a deep breath in... and out.

Again, inhale deeply, letting the air expand within you... and exhale slowly, releasing tension from your body. Let your shoulders soften. Let your jaw unclench. Let your hands rest gently. Allow your breath to slow and your mind to become quieter.

Now, imagine yourself standing at the base of a great mountain that stretches up into the clouds. A narrow path winds ahead of you, packed earth darkened by years of footsteps and scattered with small stones. It bends and disappears into the trees, beckoning you. On either side, tall evergreens rise, their many arms reaching into the air, touching the light around them. Ferns and soft moss blanket the forest floor. You feel at peace here.

Above you, the sky is a deep, luminous blue, streaked with delicate ribbons of drifting clouds. The crisp air fills your lungs—cool and clean.

The dirt path stretches before you with quiet reassurance, hinting that the climb ahead may be gentler than you expect. You sense that many others have walked here carrying pain, questions, and longing—each one seeking healing.

You have been told that at the top of this mountain is a small, wooden cabin, warmed by firelight and filled with wisdom. Inside waits a Sage—someone who knows the healing power of story and the courage it takes to tell the truth.

But to reach them, you must climb.

Take a deep breath. And begin.

You take your first step onto the path. The ground feels solid beneath you. Each step becomes an invitation to let go, to relax, to breathe in the clean air, and to reflect.

As you climb, your body feels lighter. Hope rises with each step, your shoulders easing as the weight begins to lift. You're still climbing, but the promise of meeting the Sage makes the journey feel easier.

Breathe in deeply. Exhale slowly.

Higher up the trail, the trees begin to thin. Stocky shrubs take their place, and light spills more freely across the path.

And now, you see it: a small wooden cabin nestled among pine trees and wildflowers, warm golden light spilling through the windows. Smoke curls lazily from the chimney, carrying the scent of woodsmoke on the air.

This place is safe. This is a place of healing.

You follow the path onto a wide wooden porch, where large Adirondack chairs invite you to sit and take in the view—the emerald green trees in the distance, the wildflowers nearby blooming yellow and blue. A simple sign on the door reads, *"Please enter."* You reach for the handle and step inside.

Inside, the air is warm, filled with the crackle of a fire. The walls are lined with shelves of books. A kettle hums on the stove. A soft light fills the room in a golden glow.

And there, seated in a simple wooden chair, is the Sage. They look up as you enter. Their eyes are kind. Ancient. Knowing. With a gentle gesture, they invite you to sit at the small table, where two steaming cups of tea wait.

You sit. You take a deep breath. You are fully present.

Then the Sage speaks. "What story within you still longs to be told? What needs healing?"

Let the answer rise.

Maybe it's a memory. A moment. A relationship.

A version of yourself you've tried to forget.

A truth you've never written.

A hope you thought you lost.

The Sage leans forward, voice quiet but certain: "You have the power to heal from this. You will learn as you explore it through your writing. And in doing so, you may help others heal too. You have an important story. What is the bigger question you need to answer in writing about this?"

You take a moment. You ponder this question. Then you lift the cup before you and take a slow sip.

Then the Sage reaches across the table and places something in your hands: a small, worn key. Old, warm, alive with quiet power. It's a reminder that the key to your story is one you hold in yourself.

You close your fingers around the key. The Sage smiles.

You thank the Sage and step outside, closing the door gently behind you. The world stretches wide before you. Holding the key, you begin the descent down the mountain. Yet something within you has shifted. You carry with you the memory of what must be written, the reminder that writing can heal, and the gift of a key to guide you toward deeper truths.

With each step, your body feels lighter, your spirit more grounded. The air seems clearer, the path steadier. As you continue down the mountain, take time to consider your story. What does it mean to you? How might it bring healing—to yourself, and perhaps to others as well?

When you're ready, come back to your current environment and feel free to start writing.

*

In the next chapter, I'll explore how to overcome writer's block—a challenge many writers face, especially when tackling difficult subjects. It's a common and natural part of the creative process, and approaching it with compassion can help you move through it.

Chapter 11: Overcoming Writer's Block with Compassion

"We should write, above all, because we are writers, whether we call ourselves that or not." — Julia Cameron

Almost every writer has faced the dreaded writer's block: staring at a blank page or screen, feeling that creeping sense of dread, and wondering, *What am I going to write?* At times in my writing life, I've sat down with a clear idea and the words flowed effortlessly. But there have also been times when I felt completely stuck, questioning whether I had anything left to say. *What if I'd already exhausted all my ideas? What if I'd somehow lost my ability to write? What if there was nothing more inside me?*

What makes writer's block so insidious is that it often feeds on itself. The longer I've stared at that empty page, the worse it seems to get. Frustration leads to doubt, and that can lead to paralysis.

I know I'm not alone in this experience. Many of my writing friends describe the same feelings—frustration, shame, and inadequacy. But what if writer's block isn't a sign that something is wrong with you? What if it's not a failure, but a signal? What if it's your mind or heart asking for something—a pause, a new perspective, or a reminder of why you write?

In this chapter, I'll explore writer's block as more than an obstacle. With self-compassion instead of criticism, it can become an opportunity for growth. I'll look at common causes, share practical strategies for moving through it, and as always, show how kindness toward yourself can help you reconnect with your creativity.

Anne E. Beall, PhD

What Is Writer's Block Really?

Writer's block isn't laziness, and it's not a sign that you aren't a real writer. It's a natural part of the creative process. It often occurs when something inside you needs care or attention. Researchers Ahmed and Güss found that the most common causes of writer's block are physiological, motivational, and cognitive. Writer's block often stems from things like:

- Stress, intense emotions, or illness that make it hard to think clearly.
- Fear of judgment or failure.
- Perfectionism.
- Insufficient planning.
- Emotional burnout or exhaustion.
- Losing connection with the joy or purpose of your writing.
- Avoiding something uncomfortable in your story or process.
- Needing more time for ideas to percolate.

When you see writer's block as a signal, you can meet it with curiosity. Instead of pushing yourself harder or criticizing yourself, try asking: *What do I need right now to move forward—even just a little?*

Why Self-Compassion Is the Key to Moving Forward

Writer's block often stems from the fear that what you write won't be good enough. Self-compassion can help quiet that fear. It reminds you that imperfection is part of the process—that first drafts, second drafts, and even eighty-seventh drafts are rarely perfect. When you give yourself permission to write badly, you

The Compassionate Writer

release the pressure that holds you back. The goal isn't to be flawless; it's to keep writing.

Self-compassion also helps you reconnect with joy. When writing starts to feel like a chore or a test, it's easy to forget what drew you to it in the first place. Compassion allows you to step back and remember the curiosity, creativity, and sense of wonder that made you want to write. Rather than fixating on perfection or fear of rejection, you can return to the simple pleasure of putting words on the page.

There are also times when writer's block is your mind's way of asking for a pause. Self-compassion creates space for rest and reflection. It gives you permission to honor your need for quiet, rather than forcing yourself to produce when you're not ready. Sometimes, stepping away is exactly what's needed to solve a problem or gain clarity. The answer may come to you when you least expect it.

And finally, self-compassion can remind you that you don't have to face writing challenges alone. Blockages may be a quiet signal inviting you to seek support or a new perspective. Maybe you need a trusted writer to help untangle a tricky section, or a friend to point out what's already working—even if you can't see it yet. Writing is often solitary, but it doesn't have to be isolating. Allowing yourself to reach out can sustain your creativity and deepen your work.

Anne E. Beall, PhD

Practical Strategies for Overcoming Writer's Block with Compassion

There are many ways to approach writer's block, but the worst response is to get upset, doubt that you're a "real" writer, or quit altogether. Researchers Ahmed and Güss found that the most effective remedies include taking breaks to rest and reset the mind, switching to a different project to regain momentum, and writing freely without worrying about quality. They also learned that talking with others and seeking feedback can spark clarity, new insights, and restore motivation. These findings suggest that flexibility, self-kindness, and staying connected to the act of writing itself are key to moving through creative blocks.

Write Without Judgment

One of the biggest barriers to writing is the belief that every word on the page must be brilliant. It's not a realistic expectation. Compassionate writing allows you to embrace the messiness of the creative process and give yourself some grace.

My father once told me, "You can edit a bad first draft, but you can't edit a blank page." No matter how uncertain I felt about my writing, he encouraged me to write anyway. Even bad writing, he believed, has value. It could lead to new ideas, reveal unexpected directions, or highlight areas that needed more research or reflection. And perhaps most importantly, it did one crucial thing: it got me writing. And isn't that what matters most? Just write.

The Compassionate Writer

Lower the Stakes

Sometimes, writer's block comes from putting too much pressure on a particular project or idea. Compassion means giving yourself permission to let go of those high stakes and write something purely for fun or exploration. Not everything you write will get published, and it doesn't have to. Some writing exists simply to give you joy, to spark curiosity, or to take you someplace unexpected. Just writing can become a stepping-stone, strengthening your voice and carrying you closer to the stories you want to tell.

Transition to Another Writing Project

If you feel stuck with your current project, try shifting your focus to something else. Working on a different piece of writing can help you regain momentum and rebuild your confidence. Sometimes, simply finishing a paragraph or making progress on a smaller task can reignite you. And often, stepping away from the project that's stymied you gives your mind the space it needs to return with a fresh perspective.

Embrace Rest and Recharge

If you're feeling emotionally or creatively depleted, pushing yourself to write can sometimes make things worse. Self-compassion means recognizing when you need to step away and allow yourself time to recharge. Here are some tips on how to do this:

- Take a walk, go for a jog, or tend to your garden; pay attention to the sights, sounds, and smells around you.
- Read a book or watch a movie that inspires you.

- Journal about your feelings without worrying about structure or coherence.
- Do something creative that isn't writing, like drawing, cooking, or playing music.

Remember, rest is part of the creative process—not a detour from it. Often your mind continues working in the background, so when you return to the page, you may find the solution is there waiting for you.

Reconnect with Your Purpose

When you feel stuck, it's helpful to return to the reason you write in the first place. What called you to the page? Was it a longing to make sense of your own experiences, a desire to entertain, or the hope of reaching someone who might need your words? What truths or stories do you want to tell?

Taking time to reflect on these questions can bring clarity and energy back to your practice. Remembering your deeper purpose reminds you that writing is not only about the number of words you write. It's about expressing something meaningful, whether to yourself or to others. Even in moments of doubt, this connection to purpose can help you move forward with renewed passion.

The Compassionate Writer

A Compassionate Mindset for Writer's Block

In addition to practical strategies, cultivating a compassionate mindset can help with writer's block. Here are a few guiding ideas to keep in mind that can reduce frustration and keep self-criticism in check.

Remember: Every Writer Struggles

It's easy to feel like you're the only one struggling when you hit writer's block—but you're not. Every writer, no matter how experienced, faces moments of doubt, frustration, and stretches when the words just won't come. I once worked on a piece for several years because I couldn't seem to get it right. I kept returning to it, revising again and again. If I had to guess, I'd say I went through more than thirty drafts before it finally came together.

Trust the Seasons of Creativity

Creativity has its own rhythms, much like the seasons. There are times when the words come easily and times when they feel stuck. Trust that the "winter" of writer's block will eventually give way to the "spring" of inspiration. As Megan Baxter writes:

> "Now, I allow myself to write seasonally. Spring comes with sugaring, then seeding, and summer with planting, harvesting, and market days, then fall with storing, logging, and cleaning; I let creativity lope around the edges of my mind. But when the ground freezes up, and the snow falls, and all the wood is split and stacked, the seeds ordered for next year's fields it comes to me. This feels natural here on the farm, unforced."

Celebrate Small Wins

Progress doesn't have to look like finishing a chapter or a draft. Writing a single sentence, brainstorming an idea, or even jotting down a few notes can be a victory. Celebrate these small steps because they're part of the journey.

Believe in Yourself

One thing I've learned is this: you can do what you believe you can do—and you can't do what you believe you can't. That might sound trite, but it's not. There's a wealth of psychological research showing how our beliefs can either limit us or propel us forward. I've always believed in the power of affirmations, and my personal one is simple: *I can do it.* Whenever I start to doubt myself, I remind myself that I've done hard things before—and I can do this, too. So believe in yourself. And if you catch yourself thinking *I can't,* stop and remind yourself: *Yes, I can.*

Exercise: The Ten-Minute Freewrite

Set a timer for ten minutes and write whatever comes to mind. Don't worry about structure, grammar, or the quality of your prose. Just put words down, even if they seem nonsensical or repetitive. The goal is to release the pressure to be "good" and simply get back into the rhythm of writing.

Exercise: Write Something "Useless"

Take a break from your main project and write something completely unimportant—maybe a silly poem, a scene you'll never use, or a character you find amusing. Describe whatever's in front of you right now: a tree, a cat, a fleck of dust, a hairbrush, a salt shaker on your table. Make up a story for it. Or write about a small, recent moment—forgetting your keys, putting your shirt on backwards. Let it be light, throwaway, playful. By lowering the stakes, you create space to rediscover the joy of writing—without the pressure to get it "right."

Exercise: Overcoming Feelings of Being Overwhelmed

Writer's block often shows up when we're feeling overwhelmed—when the to-do list feels endless, the pressure is high, and it seems impossible to make progress. That's also when the inner critic speaks the loudest. For me, those are the moments when I start to spiral: *I'm not doing enough. I'll never catch up. I'm wasting my time. This should be easier.*

One of the most effective ways to calm this storm is to give those feelings a place to land on the page. Take a blank sheet of paper and draw a line down the middle. On the **left side**, write down all the overwhelming thoughts, emotions, and inner-critic statements running through your head. Be honest, even if what comes up feels irrational or dramatic. For example:

- "I just can't seem to get anything done."
- "I don't have the energy for this."
- "No one likes what I write."
- "I should have a best-selling novel by now, with all the time I've put into this."
- "I'm just not any good at this."

Then, on the **right side**, write calm, rational responses to each of those thoughts. Talk back to the inner critic. Below is an example.

Thoughts/emotions/inner-critic statements	Rational responses to each thought
"I just can't seem to get anything done."	"I wrote two pages yesterday and revised a paragraph that I had been stuck on for weeks."
"I don't have the energy for this."	"I've managed to write at least a little each week. Writing takes time, and I have shown I do have the energy for this."
"No one likes what I write."	"I got positive feedback on my last piece, and even if not everyone connects with my work, it still matters."
"I should have a best-selling novel by now, with all the time I've put into this."	"Very few people have best-selling novels, and it can take years to hone one's craft. Writing takes time."
"I'm just not any good at this."	"I've come a long way with my writing, and I've improved a lot. I'm proud of my progress and I'm getting better."

When you're done, you'll have a clear and grounded response to each anxious or self-critical thought. This simple act can be surprisingly powerful—it shifts you from emotional overload into clarity and self-compassion. And chances are, you'll feel lighter, calmer, and more able to return to the page.

The Compassionate Writer

Exercise: A Compassionate Writer's Manifesto

Create a manifesto for how you'll approach writing with compassion, especially during moments of struggle. Your manifesto might include affirmations and understanding statements like:

- "I give myself permission to write imperfectly."
- "I can do this!"
- "Rest is part of my creative process."
- "I believe in myself."
- "I trust that inspiration will return when it's ready."
- "I know I have an important story to tell."
- "I celebrate every small step I take toward my goals."

Write your manifesto somewhere you'll see it often and use it as a reminder to treat yourself with kindness throughout your writing journey.

Writing Prompts

Reconnecting with Purpose and Joy

- Write a love letter to your creativity. Not your productivity. Not your discipline. Just your creativity—your strange, sacred spark.
- Write about the reasons you began writing and what it gives you beyond publishing. How does it support or sustain you? In what ways has it made you a better person? What lessons has it taught you along the way?

When You Feel Overwhelmed or Frozen

- Describe a time when not writing was the right choice. What did the stillness give you? How did it change the way you came back to the page?

Permission to Play

- Take a cliché writing rule ("show, don't tell" or "write every day") and write a satirical guide explaining why it's absurd.

Letters to the Self

- Write a letter to yourself from the version of you who never stopped writing. What encouragement do you offer? What do you remind yourself?

Writing as Rest and Restoration

- Write a scene where a character finds a hidden garden that belongs only to them. What grows there? What words are etched on the stones?

Unlocking Flow Again

- Begin with the line: "I don't know what I want to say, but…" and write freely for ten minutes. Follow every thought. No editing. No censoring. Do not cross anything out. Just write without thinking. Let your voice flow.

Build a "Creative First Aid Kit"

- Make a list of five items, quotes, rituals, or mantras that soothe your creative anxiety. Keep this somewhere visible when you're blocked.

The Compassionate Writer

Guided Visualization: A Visit to Writer's Haven

Take a moment to sit comfortably, allowing your body to relax into the surface beneath you. Inhale deeply, filling your lungs with air, then exhale slowly. Take another deep breath, this time deeper, and exhale even more slowly. Feel the tension leaving your shoulders, neck, and back as you settle into the surface that is supporting you. Take one last deep breath and release it slowly.

Now, imagine walking along a quaint cobblestone street in the heart of a small, peaceful village. The late afternoon sunlight filters gently through the branches of tall, leafy trees that line the street, creating dappled shadows along the ground. A soft breeze brushes against your skin, carrying with it the delicate scent of lavender.

Small, brightly painted houses line both sides of the street. You notice a salmon-colored home with cheerful white shutters, an azure cottage with cascading flower boxes spilling over with petunias, and a pale grey house trimmed with sparkling red geraniums. As you walk, you marvel at how carefully each house has been designed—no two are alike.

Soon, you come to a house painted in your favorite color. It feels as though it was made just for you. The front porch is framed by flowering vines, and the white trim gleams in the warm sunlight. On the door is a beautifully engraved wooden sign that reads:

"Writer's Haven: A Sanctuary for Creativity. All Writers Welcome. Please come in!"

You smile at the invitation and step onto the wooden porch, noticing how the floorboards creak softly beneath you. The scent of freshly baked bread drifts through the door. You take a deep breath, letting the soothing aroma calm you.

With a gentle pull, you open the door. A soft bell chimes as it swings shut behind you. The interior is cozy and inviting. A hearth with a crackling fire lies at the end of a cozy living room. Plush, overstuffed armchairs, a rocking chair, and a cozy couch encircle the hearth. Shelves overflowing with books line the walls.

From upstairs, a soothing voice calls down. "Welcome to Writer's Haven. This is a place for writers to reconnect with themselves, especially when they feel stuck. Take your time. Everything you need is here."

You settle into a deep armchair by the fire. The soft crackling of the flames fills the room as you take a moment to reflect on your writing.

You start to ponder a few questions: Am I feeling burnt out? Do I need to take a break from my writing to recharge my creative energy? Am I pushing myself too hard or setting unrealistic expectations? Or is there something deeper beneath my writer's block—fear, doubt, or perfectionism?

Allow the answers to come to you naturally. Don't force them; just sit with the questions and trust that the insights will rise in their own time.

When you're ready, you rise from the armchair and make your way to a staircase near the front door. The wooden stairs creak softly as you ascend to the second floor, where you find a door with a plaque that reads: *"Inspiration."*

You open the door and step inside. The air feels alive, humming faintly with possibility. A soft, golden yellow fills the room, creating an atmosphere that is both calming and energizing.

The Compassionate Writer

At the far end of the room, tall windows overlook a rose garden with flowers of different colors. You go over to see red, pink, and yellow roses, and even a single large lavender-colored rose.

In the center of the room stands a large wooden table, and resting on it is an open book. You approach it and realize this is special. Its pages shimmer faintly, as though alive. As you lean in, you see the book has a question written in a stylized script on the page. It says:

What is really bothering you about your writing right now?

Watch as the book reveals the answer. It might appear as words on the page, as images, or as feelings that rise within you. Trust whatever arises—it is here to guide you.

When you're ready, turn the page, which is blank. Now the same cursive handwriting appears:

Are you resisting the story you want to tell? If so, what are the reasons?

Consider the question and let the answers reveal themselves on the page. You might see images, hear words, or simply feel something stir inside you. Whatever arises—an emotion, a memory, a symbol—notice it. Gently explore what it might be trying to show you.

You turn to the next page.

Is there a different perspective or approach you could take to unlock your creativity?

Once again, let the answer come to you—gently, without forcing it. The book responds in its own quiet way, offering a word, an image, a phrase. Let it guide you.

Now, take a moment to reflect on what you've learned.

As you descend to the first floor, you take one last look at the cozy living room, the crackling fire, and the inviting space. Writer's Haven is always here for you. Whenever you feel stuck, return to this place. Your creativity is never gone—it simply needs space to breathe. Now, gently return to your present moment.

*

In the next chapter, I'll explore how to edit your work with compassion—an essential step in transforming a rough draft into something truly powerful.

Chapter 12: Compassionate Editing: Balancing Criticism and Kindness

"I have rewritten—often several times—every word I have ever published. My pencils outlast their erasers." — Vladimir Nabokov

The Psychological Experience of Editing

I used to believe that great writers sat down, typed out a draft, and their first version was perfect. Because of this, I wrote quickly, often convinced that whatever I'd just finished was as good as it was ever going to get.

But time has taught me otherwise: first drafts are almost always the roughest. Editing is where the real magic happens—the stage where messy, half-formed ideas sharpen and blurry visions become polished pieces. This isn't just about fixing typos or cleaning up grammar; it's about digging into the piece and bringing some clarity to the chaos.

Still, for many writers, editing feels daunting and at times disheartening. It's often the hardest part of the process for me. Some writers thrive on revision, but I've found it stirs up deep emotions. It's a vulnerable place. I've noticed three major emotional hurdles that often show up during editing: discouragement, overwhelm, and either confusion or frustration with feedback.

Discouragement about the Quality of the Work

Seeing just how much revision a piece needs, especially when you thought it was nearly finished, can feel crushing. I've had moments where it became clear that readers didn't understand a scene, or where feedback revealed the structure needed reworking so the timeline made more sense. And that's when I think: *If this needs so much work, maybe it's not good at all.*

When I read critique group feedback or begin making line edits, my inner critic shows up pointing out every flaw and planting seeds of doubt. And I think, *If it's this bad, why even bother fixing it?* I start to feel like a fake writer—someone whose work is riddled with problems.

Feeling Overwhelmed by the Number of Revisions

Sometimes, just opening the file and facing everything that needs to be fixed feels like too much. I've received feedback on nearly every page of a manuscript—sometimes with multiple comments per page, and often from several different people. It takes time, energy, and mental clarity to go through each one and decide how or whether to address it.

I sit there, staring at the screen, overwhelmed by everything my writing still lacks. And then discouragement creeps in: *This is too much. This is going to take forever. Why even bother?* That feeling that it could take days, weeks, or even months to fix can be paralyzing.

Frustration and Confusion with Feedback

If you're part of a critique group, feedback from several people can sometimes be contradictory. One person says a scene is moving, another says it falls flat. One says cut, another says expand. I'm left wondering what I should do and which feedback is "correct."

At times, I get feedback in the form of many questions people want me to answer in the piece. *How old were you then? How old were the kids? Was this your first marriage? Had you ever experienced anything like this before?* If I respond to every question, I'll double the piece, which wasn't my intent.

I've wrestled with these frustrations, and for years I hated revising. But something has shifted. Now, I approach editing with compassion for my work and for myself. I've learned to trust my voice, even when uncertainty creeps in. In this chapter, I'll explore the art of compassionate editing and share strategies to help you stay motivated, grounded, and connected to the story you want to tell.

Types of Editing

Editing isn't just one task; it's a layered process with distinct stages, each serving a different purpose. The four primary types of editing are developmental editing, line editing, copyediting, and proofreading. Understanding how they differ can make the revision process feel more manageable and less overwhelming.

Developmental editing is all about the big picture. It asks questions like: *Does the story make sense? Are the characters fully developed? Is the pacing too fast or too slow?* This stage often involves rewriting, cutting, or reorganizing entire scenes or chapters. It can feel daunting because it forces you to zoom out and evaluate the structure of your work as a whole. But it's also where major breakthroughs happen. Sometimes, the story hiding inside the first draft finally begins to emerge here. It's messy, uncertain work, but it's also where the best foundation is built.

Line editing zooms in on the prose. It's about refining how the story is told—ensuring each sentence flows smoothly, that word choices reflect the tone and mood, and that your voice as a writer shines through. In this stage, I often find myself tightening dialogue, reworking awkward phrasing, or eliminating repetition. Line editing can be deeply satisfying because you're shaping the language into something more elegant and intentional. But it can also be exhausting; every sentence demands your full attention.

Copyediting is the most technical layer of the editing process. It focuses on grammar, punctuation, syntax, consistency, and style rules. It's less about what you're saying and more about how correctly and consistently you're saying it. This includes catching typos, fixing subject-verb agreement, checking formatting, and spotting continuity errors—like making sure a character's eye color doesn't change halfway through the book. Copyediting is crucial for polishing the work before it reaches readers. Although it's less emotionally intense than other forms of editing, it still requires a sharp focus.

Proofreading comes at the very end after all the heavy lifting is done. It's a final pass to catch any lingering typos, formatting glitches, or overlooked errors before publication or submission. It's not the time for big changes, but rather for ensuring everything is clean, polished, and professional. It's the last type of editing before the piece is released into the world.

How to Approach Editing

The truth is there's no single "right" way to edit. Some writers start with the easy fixes; others dive straight into the toughest problems. Some tackle a piece section by section, while others jump around and revise whatever grabs their attention. Everyone's process is different—and figuring out what works best for you is part of becoming a better writer.

That said, many writers find it helpful to work from big-picture issues down to the smaller details. This usually means starting with developmental edits (structure, pacing, character arcs), then moving into sentence-level work, and finally addressing copyediting and proofreading. This top-down approach helps avoid wasted effort—for example, fixing punctuation in a scene that might later get cut entirely.

Personally, I begin by evaluating how the story is taking shape—looking at structure and making sure the throughline is clear and consistent. Once the major narrative elements are working, I focus on refining the prose at the sentence level, tightening language and improving flow. Last comes copyediting and proofreading to catch grammar, punctuation, and small errors.

Although some level of editing is essential for every writer, you don't have to do it all alone. You can also hire professionals to help with different stages of editing. There are experienced developmental editors, line editors, and copy editors who can offer not only fixes but insight. And working with them can be a great learning experience that strengthens your writing for future projects.

If you find yourself consistently giving up on drafts or struggling to finish revisions, the problem might not be your writing—it might be your approach to editing. I've had times when I just couldn't face a particular piece. And that's okay. I give myself the grace to set it aside for a while. But if I believe in the piece, I don't abandon it forever—I always come back to it.

Sometimes, I just make myself sit down and start editing, even when I don't want to. I don't wait for motivation to show up. Some writers do wait, and that may work for them. But for me, it's about building a steady practice that helps me bring out the best in my work.

In the end, the process that works for you is the one that produces finished work that is ready to share with the world. Whether you edit all at once, little by little, on your own or with help—what matters most is that you keep showing up for your work.

Compassionate Approach to Editing—Five Key Mindsets

Compassionate editing is about cultivating a kinder, more supportive relationship with yourself during revision. When I approach editing with the right mindset, the process feels lighter—less like a battle. I rely on five key mindsets to help me step into the work with more ease and less resistance.

1. Imperfection is part of the process.

Even masterpieces began as flawed drafts. You're not supposed to get it right on the first try, and you shouldn't expect that. Editing is where we discover the truest version of your work.

2. Good writing takes time.

Revisions often take far longer than drafting, but that doesn't mean you're slow. It means you're doing the real work. Don't let the amount of revision convince you that you're failing.

3. Revision is a process of discovery.

Some of my best insights don't arrive in the first draft—they surface during revision, often quietly. Compassion means staying curious: What is this piece really trying to say? What else could it become? What is that spark, that vague, insistent thought trying to come through? Don't rush it. Let yourself linger in this part of the process; it can be quietly revelatory.

4. Writing is never truly finished.

Even published authors tinker with their own work at readings. Nothing is ever perfect—just the best it can be in this moment. Learn when to pause, let go, and move on.

5. You are not your draft.

This mindset is crucial. Your writing is not your worth. Treat your draft with care but remember your value doesn't hinge on a single sentence or even a single book.

I keep these five reminders printed above my desk. Whenever I feel discouraged or stuck, I return to them. Before you begin editing, or anytime the process feels overwhelming, revisit these mindsets. Let them reassure you when revision feels difficult.

The Two Sides of Editing: Critic and Creator

Editing requires you to be both the critic and the creator. The critic evaluates what needs to improve, and the creator protects the heart of the story. Compassionate editing means balancing these roles—ensuring that your critic doesn't overpower your creator, and your creator doesn't ignore what needs refining.

Tips for Nurturing the Creator

The creator's role is to preserve what already works—those moments of emotional resonance, sharp dialogue, or vivid descriptions. This side of you remembers why the story matters. Here are some suggestions for engaging the creator.

- Celebrate what's working. Highlight lines, scenes, or turns of phrase that make you feel proud or emotionally connected.

- Reconnect with your inspiration. Remind yourself: *What was my original objective?* That initial spark still matters—it propels your vision.
- Protect your voice. Be careful not to over-edit or revise to the point that your unique voice is lost. The best version of your story is one that only *you* can tell. This becomes especially important when you receive line edits from others. Remember, their suggestions should clarify and strengthen your writing, not replace your style with theirs.

Tips for Engaging the Critic Compassionately

The critic's job is to spot what isn't working—awkward sentences, inconsistent pacing, underdeveloped characters, and plot holes. This role is essential for growth, but if left unchecked, the critic can become harsh or feel paralyzing. Below are some tips for engaging the critic.

Ask specific, constructive questions. Instead of blanket judgments like "This scene is terrible," try asking yourself:

- What isn't quite working here?
- What am I really trying to say?
- How can I make this clearer?
- What would make this better?

Focus on solutions, not just problems. Treat every issue as an opportunity to improve your work. The goal is not to tear your writing down, but to strengthen it.

Compassionate editing happens when both sides—the Critic and the Creator—are balanced and in conversation. Together, they will shape your story into something stronger and truer.

The Compassionate Writer

Practical Strategies for Compassionate Editing

When you're editing, it's essential to be kind to yourself and sometimes to reconnect with the reason you wrote a piece in the first place. Here are the approaches that help me move through this process.

1. Take a Pause to Gain Perspective

Before diving into edits, give your work some breathing room. Whether it's a few days or a few weeks, stepping away allows your emotions to settle and your judgment to sharpen. Use this time to celebrate your progress—finishing a draft is no small feat.

2. Reconnect with Your Creative Purpose

Before revising, pause and ask yourself: *Why did I write this piece?* Return to the original idea, memory, or emotion that inspired you. Then, read through your draft and highlight where that shines through. Recognize that those moments are working and start from a place of strength.

3. Embrace Iteration

Great writing takes shape through many rounds of editing. Aim to improve your draft even just a little with each pass. Think of it like sculpting—each small refinement brings your story's shape into clearer focus. And don't forget to step away between rounds; taking breaks keeps your perspective fresh and your energy renewed. It's in these cycles of revision and rest that your work can truly become great.

4. Know When to Let Go

There's a moment when editing crosses the line into avoidance because you're nervous about what others will think, or you fear failure. When you find yourself endlessly revising, ask yourself:

- Have I told the story I wanted to tell?
- Does this reflect my voice and vision?
- Am I holding on to this because of fear?

When the answer is "yes," it may be time to let your work go—and share it.

5. The Last Pass

When your manuscript feels complete and you're ready for the final polish, I recommend reading it aloud. Personally, I use the read-aloud feature in Microsoft Word, and I simply listen. This is often when I notice if something feels off—an awkward phrase, a missed word, or a lingering typo. By the time I've listened through without finding anything to adjust, I know the piece is ready.

Compassion in Collaborative Editing

If you're working with an editor, critique partner, or beta reader, stay open to feedback while protecting your creative voice.

How to Approach Feedback with Compassion:

- Thank your reader or editor for their input, even if you don't agree with every suggestion.
- Remember: Feedback does not provide an evaluation of your worth as a writer.
- Take time to process feedback before deciding what to revise.

The Compassionate Writer

- Incorporate only the changes that resonate with you, but don't think you need to implement every suggestion. I use the following filters to determine which changes I want to make.
    - Will this change make the piece stronger?
    - Does this align with my vision for this piece and the story I'm trying to tell?

At *Chicago Story Press Literary Journal*, every piece goes through an editing process. Most authors are genuinely grateful to have someone engage deeply with their work, offering suggestions to refine and elevate it. I often receive heartfelt notes from writers who appreciate the care and attention taken to make their piece stronger. They understand that editing is an investment—a sign that their work is valued.

Occasionally, I encounter writers who resist any changes, feeling that their work should remain untouched. But the truth is, feedback is rarely about tearing down a piece; it's about seeing its potential. Some of the most heavily edited pieces I've worked on have grown into something extraordinary—and many of those have gone on to become the most widely read.

I'm always amazed at how much better my writing becomes after multiple rounds of revision. It takes time for a piece to truly shine—but that's part of the beauty. The longer I write, the more I see revision as a gift, not a chore. I don't love editing, but I know each pass brings me closer to the story I want to tell. And that gets me excited. It reminds me that the work is improving—and that I'm moving toward a place where I'll be ready to share it.

Anne E. Beall, PhD

Clarity is Compassion for Your Reader

Writing is, at its heart, about communication. One of the greatest acts of compassion you can offer your reader is making your story easy to follow—so they never feel confused or lost. There's nothing worse than writing that sounds smart but says nothing. We've all read something and thought, *Wait, what did I just read?*

Having compassion for your reader doesn't mean simplifying your ideas or avoiding emotional or narrative complexity. It means guiding them with enough clarity that they can follow the thread of your story with confidence. A well-told story doesn't just convey meaning—it builds trust. It invites readers to settle in, to lose themselves in the world you've created, rather than struggle to decode who's speaking, what's happening, or why it matters.

Clarity is an act of care. When your writing helps the reader feel oriented and emotionally grounded, they're free to engage more deeply.

Here's how to ensure clarity in your writing:

- Strong Story Structure—A clear beginning, middle, and end help readers feel grounded. Even experimental narratives should offer a sense of progression.
- Clean, Intentional Prose—Sentences should flow naturally and not be convoluted. If a sentence feels like a puzzle, it pulls the reader out of the experience and can make them feel stupid.
- Well-Defined Characters—Readers connect with characters whose desires, struggles, and voices are distinct. When characters blend together, act inconsistently, or all sound the same, the reader becomes less engaged in the story.

- Strong settings—Readers need a strong sense of place. They want to see characters move through their environments and understand how people and spaces interact. A vivid setting grounds the story and makes every scene feel more alive.

A compassionate writer seeks to share, to connect, and to offer something meaningful. When we craft stories that are clear, relatable, and emotionally honest, we show respect for our readers and invite them on a journey worth taking.

As you write, ask yourself:

- Am I making this story clear and understandable?
- Am I creating an experience that welcomes or overwhelms?

Writing is an act of generosity. The more we consider our readers' experience, the more deeply our stories will resonate.

Editing Prompts

The following prompts are designed to help you edit a piece you're currently working on—whether you're just getting started or nearing completion. Use them to reflect on what your story needs and how you want to shape it in revision.

Big-Picture Edits: Strengthening Structure and Story

- Summarize your piece in one sentence. Does it capture the heart of your story? If not, what's missing?
- Identify the major plot points. Are they clear, connected, and complete? Note any areas where the plot feels confusing, thin, or underdeveloped.

Character Development: Bringing Depth and Nuance

- Describe your main character's biggest internal conflict in one sentence. Does your writing clearly show this struggle throughout? If not, where can you highlight it more?
- Read through your character descriptions—are they more about physical traits or personality? Rewrite one description to focus on emotions, habits, or body language instead.

Line-Level Editing: Refining Language and Clarity

- Search your draft for words or expressions you tend to repeat. Count how often they appear, then brainstorm fresh alternatives or rephrase sentences to add variety and precision.
- Read a section aloud. Do any sentences feel awkward? Rewrite one sentence for better flow.

Final Polish: Preparing for Readers

- Read your entire piece aloud. Where do you stumble? Where does it feel awkward? Mark those places for revision.
- Identify the sentence or scene you're most proud of. What makes it work so well? Can you apply that strength to another section?

Your Approach to Editing

- Outline how you plan to approach editing in the future and make a simple checklist to keep yourself focused and organized.
- Identify which parts of the editing process feel most difficult—maybe it's receiving feedback, rewriting large

sections, or staying motivated through multiple drafts. Once you know your challenges, brainstorm ways to make them easier. You might set smaller, daily goals, break big edits into manageable tasks, or schedule short, focused editing sessions.

Guided Visualization: The Playhouse of the Draft

Find a quiet, comfortable place and sit. Take a deep breath in… and exhale slowly. Inhale again deeply, filling your lungs, and release any tension you're holding when you breathe out. Let your shoulders drop. Breathe in deeply like this several times. Feel a calmness spread through you as you relax.

Now, imagine yourself in front of a brick building with a large sign above double doors that says: *The Playhouse of the Draft*. The doors are open and twinkling lights just beyond the threshold invite you inside. You smell a scent of polished wood and the hint of sawdust.

This is where your story lives—not on paper, but in a performance. In this playhouse, your characters come to life, through actors on a stage. You will watch from the best seat in the house and be the only member of the audience. This performance is only for you. The sets are in place, the lights are warm, and the actors are ready to step into the world you've created.

You step inside the lobby, which is warm and quiet. You hear faint sounds from within—footsteps on stage, voices rehearsing lines, curtains being drawn.

Tonight, you are not the playwright, and you are not one of the actors. You are the critic—curious, discerning, fair. You've come to witness what's working… and what isn't.

You walk toward the theater, slipping quietly into the back row. The lights dim. The curtain rises. Above the stage, a sign glows softly: *The Beginning*.

The first part of your story comes to life on stage. Watch it unfold exactly as it was written. If you've written a memoir, you may see yourself portrayed by an actor; if you've created fiction, your characters step into view. Either way, they are speaking your words and moving through the world you depicted.

Observe closely. As the scene plays out, ask yourself gently: What is working, and what isn't? Take note—without judgment. This isn't about perfection. It's about clarity, growth, and truth.

The lights fade. Take a quiet moment to reflect. What feels strong? What feels unclear? Imagine yourself jotting down a few notes about what you'd like to revise. Ask yourself: *Does the beginning draw the reader in? Is the central conflict clear from the start? Do the characters feel real and believable?*

Now, the lights rise again, and the curtain opens. The sign above glows with the title: *The Middle*. Watch closely as the performance unfolds. Notice what holds your attention—and what doesn't.

When the lights fade again, pause. Imagine yourself making a few thoughtful notes. Remember: the middle is where many stories sag, and if yours does, note that. Ask yourself: *Does the pacing work? Are the stakes clear and rising? Are the characters evolving?*

Now, the lights come on, and the curtain rises. The glowing sign reads: *The Ending*. The story builds toward its final moments. Watch the characters. Listen to the dialogue. Feel the weight of everything that's come before. When it's over, ask yourself: *Does this ending feel earned and emotionally true? How would a reader feel after finishing this work?*

The Compassionate Writer

Let the answers come to you. And imagine taking a few notes about what is working and what isn't with your ending.

Now it's time to leave the theater. You make your way to the center of the grand lobby. A mirror hangs on the wall—framed in gold. You look into it and ask yourself: *What do I love about this work and what do I need to do to improve it?* Take time for the answers to come to you.

You've watched your story, and now you understand it more fully. Take one final breath in… and exhale slowly. Step back out into the night. The playhouse behind you is quiet now.

But it will be waiting. Whenever you need to revisit, rewatch, revise—its doors will be open.

*

When you have a revised draft that you feel good about, you may want to share it with a writing group. In the next chapter, I'll explore how to build a compassionate writing community—a space where you can give and receive feedback with kindness, grow as a writer, and connect with others who share your creative journey.

Chapter 13: Cultivating a Compassionate Writing Community

"Alone, we can do so little; together, we can do so much."
— Helen Keller

Writing can sometimes feel like a solitary pursuit, but it doesn't have to be. Building a compassionate writing community of people who support, encourage, and challenge you can transform your writing life.

A writing community can provide a space where you feel seen and supported, where your vulnerability is met with kindness, and where ideas and feedback can lead to your growth as a writer. A compassionate writing community is a safe, supportive environment where writers encourage one another and celebrate everyone's wins—both big and small.

In this chapter, I'll explore how to create and sustain a writing community rooted in compassion, whether through a formal critique group or an informal circle of writing friends. Over the years, I've started and run a few critique groups, and I've participated in many others. Through these experiences, I've learned what makes a writing group successful and what pitfalls to avoid.

Why Having a Community is Important

Sharing your writing can feel like standing naked in front of others and exposing a part of yourself that few people ever see. A compassionate community can provide a safe space to take risks, share imperfect drafts, and receive feedback that is encouraging and helpful. It should be a place where you can begin showing your

The Compassionate Writer

thoughts to others with confidence, knowing they will be met with respect.

I don't believe any writer, myself included, can view their own work with complete objectivity. There have been times when I thought a piece was crystal clear and polished, only to realize later that parts were confusing or needed improvement.

A supportive writing community can help you recognize both the strengths and weaknesses in your work. Feedback reveals what resonates, what's unclear, and how your writing lands with readers. After all, we write to be read. A strong community can help you assess whether your intentions—such as conveying a message, developing a character, or creating an engaging plot—are truly coming through.

These groups can also support you as you navigate the highs and lows of writing, reminding you that you're not alone in your struggles or your triumphs. That sense of shared experience matters. It's easy to get discouraged by rejections, silence, or the long grind of writing. But knowing others are facing the same challenges can make the load feel lighter and help you keep going.

Writing with others, even informally, can create a valuable sense of accountability. I know many people who are part of online writing communities where they show up simply to write—they never even share their work with the group. But the routine of writing together encourages consistency.

I participate in one of these groups myself, and I find it incredibly motivating. The woman who hosts it offers one-hour sessions at 11 a.m. Central Time on Mondays, Wednesdays, and Fridays, and we meet via Zoom. We spend a few minutes at the start catching up, then each person shares what they plan to work on.

There are usually five to eight people on any given day. At noon, we check in again and briefly share how it went. We don't read our work aloud, but simply being surrounded by other writers is deeply motivating.

What Makes a Writing Community Compassionate?

Not all writing communities are created equal. A truly supportive group is respectful, kind, and guided by clear goals. I've been part of incredible circles that nurtured me, but I've also experienced groups so discouraging that I stopped writing altogether. At the time, I didn't realize the issue was the group, not my work. That's why it's essential to choose or build a community that aligns with your needs and that truly supports you.

Kind, Constructive Feedback

Compassionate writing communities give feedback that is honest but kind, focused on helping writers grow rather than tearing them down. Critique should be specific and actionable—not vague or abstract. In the group I run, members are asked not only to identify issues in a piece but also to suggest possible ways to address them. I believe that simply pointing out flaws without offering solutions is rarely helpful.

For example, imagine being told, *"Your main character isn't believable."* That's deflating and not particularly useful. But compare it to:

> "I didn't find the main character believable because she didn't seem to care much about her husband, which struck me as odd since they've only been married a couple of years. Maybe you could show

> some earlier misgivings she has about him, or hint at deeper issues in the marriage earlier in the piece."

That kind of feedback gives the writer something to work with.

Feedback should also highlight strengths of the work. If you can't find anything positive to say about a piece, I suggest saying nothing at all.

Celebrating Each Other's Wins

In a compassionate writing community, members celebrate each other's achievements—whether it's finishing a draft, getting published, or simply overcoming writer's block. Everyone is valued equally. I've been in groups where some writers were celebrated, while others were overlooked. If you find yourself in one of those, *walk away*. A true writing community lifts *everyone* up.

A compassionate writing community recognizes that every writer is on their own journey. There's no room for comparison or envy—only encouragement and understanding. Some writers may be just beginning, while others may be close to publication. Supporting writers at different points in their journey not only strengthens the group but also fosters empathy and a deeper appreciation for the writing process as a whole.

Respecting Each Writer's Voice

Compassionate feedback respects the writer's unique voice and vision. It's not about telling someone how *you* would write their story—it's about helping them tell *their* story in the most powerful way possible. Every writer has a unique voice, and as long as that voice is clear, it's important to encourage it and let it flourish.

Anne E. Beall, PhD

How to Build or Find a Writing Community

If you don't already have a writing community, don't worry—it's never too late to find one or even build one yourself. Here are some steps to help you connect with writers and create a supportive, encouraging group.

Start with People You Know

Start by looking for writers within your existing circle—friends, colleagues, or classmates—who might be interested in forming a writing group. Even a small group of two or three can make a meaningful difference. Personally, I prefer groups with four to seven members. I've been in groups as large as twenty, and it quickly becomes overwhelming. You don't get much depth from each person, and it's harder to build trust. With four to seven people, you get a good mix of perspectives while keeping things manageable. In my current group, we meet monthly for two hours over Zoom and critique three pieces during each session. This allows about forty minutes per piece and also enables group members to submit work every other month, which they appreciate.

Join Local or Online Writing Groups

Many communities have writing groups that meet in libraries, bookstores, or community centers. Online spaces—like forums, social media groups, and writing platforms—are also great places to connect with like-minded writers. I've found writing groups through Meetup, and I've even seen them advertised at my local library.

The Compassionate Writer

Attend Writing Workshops or Conferences

Workshops and conferences offer opportunities to meet other writers who share your interests and goals. These events can be a great way to build connections and find potential critique partners. I've found writing groups through workshops and formed lasting friendships with writers I met at conferences. You can find many writing workshops and conferences online.

Be Intentional About Who You Invite

When building a writing group, focus on finding people who share your values—especially a commitment to kindness and constructive feedback. Look for writers who are open-minded, respectful, and eager to support each other. Talk to potential members about how they approach critiques and be clear about what your group is—and what it isn't. Make sure everyone understands that members are expected to both submit work and provide feedback, and clarify whether you're looking for written critiques, oral feedback, or both.

Tips for Creating a Compassionate Writing Group

Once you've found your community, it's important to set a tone of compassion and collaboration. Here are some tips for fostering a supportive environment:

Establish Ground Rules

Before diving into critiques, set clear expectations for how the group will operate. Consider rules like:

- Respect each other's voice: Avoid imposing your own style or preferences on someone else's work.

- Balance praise and critique: Offer constructive suggestions alongside positive feedback.
- Be specific and actionable: Vague feedback like "I didn't like this" isn't helpful. Explain why and then offer ideas for improvement.
- Confidentiality: Respect each member's privacy by keeping shared work and discussions within the group.
- Appoint a consistent group leader: This person moderates every session, sets the tone, manages time, and ensures discussions remain respectful and balanced. They're also responsible for addressing any issues that arise and making sure feedback includes both praise and constructive critique. In the groups I run, that leader is me.
- Time limits: Set time limits for each person's critique so everyone participates equally.

Read a Preamble before Each Meeting

I conduct a monthly critique group for memoir writers. To ensure we maintain a respectful and productive space, I begin each meeting by reading a preamble that outlines our group's guidelines. Here's the one I use:

"Welcome to the Critique Group! We're delighted to have you here. Our goal is to enhance each other's creative nonfiction through thoughtful, constructive, and respectful feedback. Because these pieces often contain deeply personal stories, it's essential that we approach critiques with sensitivity and care.

The Compassionate Writer

These are our group guidelines:

- **Respectful and Encouraging**: It takes courage to share personal stories. Every memoir is a reflection of lived experience and should be treated with the utmost respect.
- **Safe**: This is a safe space where we support each other as both writers and individuals.
- **Confidential**: All submitted work is confidential and should not be shared outside the group.
- **Content Warnings**: If a piece contains sensitive material (e.g., violence, explicit content), please provide a content warning. Members may opt out of critiquing such content without judgment.
- **Constructive Feedback**: Critiques should be actionable and supportive. Each critique is limited to three to five minutes and should start with an overall positive comment before offering specific suggestions for improvement.
- **Receiving Feedback**: Writers should listen with an open mind and a closed mouth during critiques. While all feedback is a gift, it is up to the writer to decide what to incorporate.
- **Balanced Participation**: Members who submit work for critique must also provide thoughtful feedback on others' writing.
- **Oral and Written Feedback**: Please participate in the group discussion, then follow up with written comments. Your written feedback can include overall impressions, any parts of the piece that were unclear, and areas you particularly enjoyed. Feel free to include line edits if you'd like—they're always appreciated but not required.

By following these guidelines, we can create a space where all members grow as memoir writers. Thank you for being part of this journey. Let's help each other tell our stories in the most compelling way possible."

How to Give Compassionate Feedback

Use the Sandwich Method for Feedback

This approach helps balance critique with encouragement and promotes a positive, growth-oriented atmosphere:

- Start with strengths: Highlight what's working well in the piece—what you enjoyed, what stood out, and what the writer is doing effectively.
- Offer constructive critique: Focus on specific areas that could be improved. Frame your comments as opportunities and offer concrete suggestions for how the writer might address them.
- End on a positive note: Reaffirm the writer's potential and return to the strengths of the piece to leave them encouraged and motivated.
- Important: If you genuinely can't find anything positive to say, it's better to hold back than to deliver a completely negative critique. All writers need encouragement to grow—harsh feedback with no support can be deeply discouraging and unproductive.

Providing a critique doesn't mean sugarcoating or avoiding difficult truths. It means delivering feedback with care and respect, focusing on growth rather than judgment.

The Compassionate Writer

When offering feedback, keep these principles in mind:
- Focus on the work, not the writer: Feedback should always be directed at the writing itself—not the writer. Avoid language that feels personal, judgmental, or emotionally charged.
- Avoid personal critiques or life commentary: This is a writing group, not a therapy session. Please don't offer interpretations of a writer's choices as reflections of their personal life, and never critique someone's values or decisions. Our focus is on improving the craft, not analyzing the person behind it.
- Offer suggestions as options: Frame your feedback as possibilities, not prescriptions. Offering multiple ways to address a concern empowers writers to make their own choices. Phrasing feedback as a question can be especially helpful. For example:
    - "This felt a bit abrupt—what if the scene started later, in the middle of the action?"
    - "The dialogue sounds a little formal—would using more age-specific phrasing help make it sound more natural?"

Anne E. Beall, PhD

How to Receive Feedback with Compassion

Receiving feedback can be difficult because it can make you question your abilities as a writer. However, it's a vital part of growth. Here's how to approach it with compassion:

- Separate Yourself from Your Work: A critique is about improving the writing, not judging your worth as a writer.
- Listen Before Reacting: Resist the urge to defend your work right away. Take time to absorb the comments and reflect on how well they align with your goals.
- Look for Patterns: If multiple readers point out the same issue, it's worth considering. That said, trust your instincts—you don't have to implement every suggestion. It's your work, and the final decision is yours.
- Show Gratitude: Thank your readers for their time and insights, even if you don't agree with all of their feedback. A positive, open attitude fosters stronger relationships and more productive discussions.

One way to guide feedback is to include specific questions at the top of your piece. Let readers know what you're looking for, such as: *Is the dialogue working? Does this character feel flat? Is the scene clear, and is it obvious that it takes place after the wedding?* Asking questions of your critique partners can help you receive the most useful responses.

The Compassionate Writer

Do Not Tolerate Bad Behavior

One thing you should never tolerate is a group member who tears anyone down. If someone can't offer positive or constructive feedback, they don't belong in the group. Writing is challenging enough—you don't deserve to feel deflated or diminished. You deserve to be encouraged, supported, and respected.

I've had my share of negative experiences, especially in writing workshops where poor leadership allowed unhelpful feedback and even personal attacks to go unchecked. It's worth noting that writing workshops and ongoing writing groups are quite different. Workshops are often short-term—maybe a few hours, a weekend, or a single week. You share your work with people you often don't meet again. Because there's no long-term relationship or accountability, the tone can vary wildly depending on who's in charge.

In contrast, writing groups are ongoing. You build trust over time, which creates a space for honest yet respectful feedback. If you're starting or joining a writing group, prioritize kindness, clarity, and consistency. And if someone crosses the line into cruelty or condescension, don't hesitate to step away. In my experience, the harshest critics often have the least helpful feedback.

If you've created a group and are serving as the moderator, consider speaking privately with any member whose behavior may be affecting the group dynamic. It's important to address concerns directly but with empathy, helping the person understand how their actions may be coming across to others. Often, people aren't aware of the impact they're having. However, if the behavior continues and begins to compromise the safety or cohesion of the group, it may be necessary to let them know the group is no longer a good fit.

Another Option: Trusted Readers

Instead of joining a larger group, consider finding one or two trusted individuals to give you feedback. These people might be fellow writers or simply thoughtful readers who understand and appreciate your goals. Many writers rely on spouses or close friends to be both honest and gentle. When you find the right person, you'll instinctively know: they're able to highlight the strengths and weaknesses in your writing while delivering feedback with sensitivity. Most importantly, you can trust their judgment.

Trust Yourself

Ultimately, the person you must trust most is yourself. If you believe a piece is strong and feel that the criticism you receive is unfair or misses the point, honor your instincts. You are the writer. If your work says what you want it to say, respect that. For example, I once had someone in a writing group tell me that my memoir piece wasn't suitable as an essay and should be rewritten as a poem instead. She even rewrote it as a poem. Not helpful and not appreciated.

I recently attended a writing retreat and shared a deeply personal piece about the challenges of being a stepmother. Several women responded negatively. They said the piece wasn't persuasive, although they couldn't explain exactly why. It became clear they didn't want to confront their own biases about stepmothers. They didn't want to believe that the negative cultural stereotypes they held might be rooted in something real.

Their feedback told me something important: I would have an uphill battle persuading others with my piece. But it also told me I had struck a nerve. And that was what mattered.

The Compassionate Writer

I've known more than a few writers who have ignored criticism they didn't agree with. They believed in their work, and when it was rejected, they kept submitting it anyway. I even know a couple of writers who accidentally sent the same piece—unchanged—to a journal that had previously rejected it. The second time, it was accepted. Same piece. Different timing. In one case, even the same reader. Good thing they didn't revise it.

Exercise: Define What You Want from a Writing Community

Take a moment to reflect on what you're looking for in a writing community. Do you need encouragement to write more, perhaps someone who will write alongside you for accountability? Or are you seeking thoughtful critique and feedback to help improve your work? Maybe you want a group that actively celebrates each other's wins, or one that simply offers motivation and support. Make a list of everything you'd like in a writing group, then narrow it down to your top three priorities. Identifying what matters most will help you find—or build—the right community for your writing journey.

Guided Visualization: The Writer's Circle

Take a deep breath in… and out. Again, inhale deeply, filling your lungs with fresh air, and exhale, releasing any tension. Let your shoulders drop, let your mind quiet, and allow yourself to settle into this moment.

Now, imagine yourself stepping through a magnificent stone archway. You walk forward into a vast, open-air courtyard filled with golden light. The space is expansive yet welcoming, enclosed by high stone walls and lined with graceful columns that support delicate archways along the perimeter. Overhead, the sky stretches wide with a few stray clouds dancing overhead. The air carries the subtle scent of jasmine and citrus.

Ahead of you, at the courtyard's center, a grand round table stands, its smooth, polished surface glowing softly as if lit from within. Around it, writers are gathered, seated in an eclectic mix of chairs—some carved from dark mahogany, others gleaming with brass or softened with plush velvet. No two chairs are alike, yet together they form a perfect circle, as if designed for the unique individuals who occupy them. Some writers are deep in quiet thought, their fingers tapping against the arms of their chairs. Others lean in, engaged in animated conversation.

This is not a place of solitude. It is a space alive with creativity, where voices mingle and ideas take shape. You are not alone here.

As you take another step forward, a warm voice greets you.

"Welcome. We've been waiting for you."

You see the writers at the table looking up, their eyes filled with recognition, as if they already know you and understand why you're here. One by one, they make space for you in their circle, offering a seat at the table.

You look around at the faces of these writers and see compassion and understanding. These are people who know the joy and struggle of writing. Here, you will find support, encouragement, and understanding. You belong here. A soft bell chimes, signaling the start of the gathering. The writers begin to share their work.

And then, it is your turn. You take a deep breath, the weight of your words settling before you speak. Perhaps you share a story you love, or a passage you're unsure about. Perhaps you admit that you've been stuck, that the words haven't been coming as easily as they once did.

The Compassionate Writer

Consider what you want to hear from this group. Maybe you just want encouragement. Perhaps you want help with something specific. Or maybe you just want to feel accepted. Maybe you want criticism for anything that isn't quite working.

Think about what you want this group to do for you. And then see them do that. Envision the kind of feedback and the kind of group you want. See it happening right there.

You breathe in, feeling lighter. You realize you are not alone. You never were.

Slowly, the gathering comes to a close. Writers rise from their chairs and drift off through the archways.

Take a deep breath in… and out. Take a moment to reflect: what would a Writers' Circle look like for you? How can you bring this type of community into your real writing life?

You are a writer. You are already part of this circle.

*

In the next chapter, I'll discuss how to keep going in the midst of rejection and how you can cultivate resilience as a writer.

Chapter 14: Rejection and Resilience: Using Compassion to Keep Going

"Chicken Soup for the Soul was rejected by 144 publishers. If we had given up after 100 publishers, I likely would not be where I am now. I encourage you to reject rejection. If someone says no, just say NEXT!" — Jack Canfield

Rejection is one of the hardest parts of being a writer. No matter how much experience you have or how many pieces you've published, that email with *"We regret to inform you..."* still stings. You pour your heart into a piece, revise and polish it, summon the courage to send it out into the world... only to be met with a "no." It's disheartening. It can make you question your talent, your story, even your voice.

But rejection isn't failure. It's part of the process—for every writer, at every level. I've experienced countless rejections, but I've also had a few acceptances. That's the reality of a writer's life: persistence in the face of uncertainty.

Most literary magazines accept only 1–5% of submissions. Agents receive thousands of queries every year and sign only a handful of new clients. Publishing houses reject the majority of manuscripts they receive—often for reasons that have little to do with the quality of the writing. Even bestselling authors began their journeys with rejection.

J.K. Rowling's *Harry Potter and the Sorcerer's Stone* was rejected by twelve publishers. Stephen King's *Carrie* was turned down thirty times. Agatha Christie endured four years of rejection before publishing her first book. And it's even harder today.

The Compassionate Writer

In this chapter, we'll explore how to face rejection with compassion instead of self-criticism. By shifting your mindset, understanding the different types of rejection, and using concrete strategies to process and learn from it, you can keep moving forward—not just despite rejection, but because of it.

Why Rejection Feels So Personal (And Why It's Not)

When a piece of writing is rejected, it's easy to believe it reflects something about you—that you're not good enough, not talented enough to be published. But rejection is rarely that simple.

What Rejection Actually Means:

- It wasn't the right fit. Even great stories don't always match a publication's needs, tone, or specific themes.
- It wasn't the right time. Editors and agents might love your work but already have something too similar or it's not the right time of year (that Santa Claus story might be great, but it's June).
- Publishing is highly competitive. Even excellent writing gets rejected due to space limitations and editorial preferences.

What Rejection Doesn't Mean:

- That your work isn't valuable.
- That you will never be published.
- That you should stop writing.

Rejection isn't an evaluation of your worth—it's just one person's decision at one moment in time.

As a publisher of creative nonfiction, I often have to reject submissions that are excellent—well-written, compelling, and completely worthy of publication. Many of these pieces would be a great fit for *Chicago Story Press Literary Journal*, but unfortunately, I simply can't publish every great story. If I accepted everything that deserved to be published, I'd be publishing thousands of pieces, which isn't possible. I try to convey this in the rejection letters I send, but I know that receiving a rejection is still disappointing.

What often sets the published pieces apart isn't just the quality of the writing—it's the angle, topic, or perspective. Many excellent submissions cover experiences we see frequently, such as the death of a parent, and although these are deeply meaningful, they may not feel new to editors who read dozens of similar stories. That's one reason some journals eventually stop accepting certain themes. What I look for are pieces that either explore a less common subject or offer a fresh, unexpected perspective on a familiar one. Those are the stories that tend to stand out and ultimately get published.

Types of Rejections (And How to Read Them with Compassion)

Not all rejections are equal. Learning to interpret them can help you grow as a writer and view rejection as a form of progress rather than failure. Most publishers, literary journals, and many agencies follow a multi-stage review process. Initial readers often sort submissions into three categories: rejections, maybes, and acceptances.

Rejections typically go out first, while the "maybes" and strong contenders move on to additional readers or editorial discussions. This is one reason acceptances can take longer—they often require multiple rounds of review and deliberation. With so many excellent pieces competing for a limited number of slots, even strong work can end up being declined. That's why understanding the kind of rejection you've received can offer valuable insight and encouragement, rather than discouragement.

The Form Rejection (The Most Common Type)

"Thank you for submitting, but unfortunately, we are unable to accept your work at this time."

What it means: Your piece wasn't the right fit, but this doesn't reflect on its quality. Magazines, agents, and publishers send hundreds of these every day.

How to respond with compassion: Responding to rejection with compassion starts with a simple reminder: every writer experiences rejections—even the most successful ones. It is not a reflection of your talent or potential; it's simply part of the process. Instead of dwelling on it, log the rejection, acknowledge your effort, and move forward by submitting your work elsewhere. Each rejection brings you one step closer to finding the right home for your writing.

The Encouraging Rejection

"We enjoyed your submission, but it's not the right fit for us. However, we encourage you to consider us in the future."

What it means: They see potential in your work and might be interested in future submissions.

How to respond with compassion: Receiving an encouraging rejection is a positive step forward. Instead of feeling discouraged, celebrate the fact that they seem open to your work. This suggests that with persistence, your work may find the right home.

You might also consider seeking feedback on your rejected piece before sending it elsewhere. A few thoughtful revisions based on outside input might make a big difference.

Anne E. Beall, PhD

The Personalized Rejection

"We loved your piece—or a character, specific theme, lyrical prose—but we had to pass this time. We'd love to see more work from you."

What it means: Your work was seriously considered. The editor or agent is not just being polite—they genuinely connected with something in your piece. A specific compliment means your writing stood out, and they see real potential in you.

How to respond with compassion: Take this as a clear win—you're on the right track. Personalized rejections are rare, and they often mean you were *seriously considered*. You should absolutely consider submitting to the same publication in the future. Editors often develop ongoing relationships with writers this way, which can lead to eventual publication. When you submit again, mention the previous response in your cover letter—it shows you're thoughtful, professional, and committed to growth.

Don't Get Sucked into the Rejection Vortex

If you're submitting your work regularly, odds are you'll face far more rejection than acceptance. Over time, this can start to feel like a message: that you're not good enough, that your writing doesn't matter, or that the publishing world has collectively decided you have nothing valuable to say.

If most of the responses you receive are rejections, it's easy to believe they represent some larger consensus about your worth as a writer. They don't. What they reflect, more often than not, is the brutal math of supply and demand. There are too many submissions and not enough available spots. Editors reject great work every day—not because it isn't good, but because they're limited in space, timing, or editorial direction.

Another trap is the *self-fulfilling prophecy*. If you begin to believe you're destined to fail, that belief can start to shape your behavior—whether by making you send out work less often, revise less carefully, or give up altogether. Psychologist Robert Merton, who first coined the term, showed how expectations can influence outcomes simply by altering how we act. In the context of writing, this means that giving in to discouragement might actually create the failure you feared in the first place.

So resist the pull of the rejection vortex. Don't treat rejection as a verdict—it's not. Take your wins, however small they may feel, and let them guide you forward. Keep writing. Keep sending your work out. Rejection is not a reflection of your talent or potential—it's just a reflection of an overcrowded system.

Reframing Rejection: Shifting from Defeat to Growth

Instead of seeing rejection as some type of final pronouncement, try to reframe it as part of your journey as a writer. Here are some ways you can reframe rejections.

The Rejection Log

Keep a document where you track:
- What you submitted.
- Where you submitted it.
- The type of rejection you received.

This helps you see rejection as progress—proof that you're actively submitting your work.

Anne E. Beall, PhD

Submittable and Duotrope

If you're looking for places to submit your work—especially to literary magazines, contests, and small publishers—two excellent resources to explore are Submittable and Duotrope.

Submittable is a popular online submission manager used by thousands of journals, publishers, and contests. You'll need to create a free account to submit, and once you do, you can track the status of your submissions. It's especially helpful for staying organized, as it keeps a record of what you've sent where.

Duotrope, on the other hand, is a searchable database of literary markets. It requires a small monthly or annual fee, but offers robust search filters, submission trackers, and data on response times and acceptance rates. It's ideal for researching potential homes for your work—whether you're submitting fiction, nonfiction, or poetry.

Many writers use both tools: Duotrope to research where to submit and Submittable to send the work. Together, they can demystify the process and help you approach submissions with more confidence and efficiency.

The Rejection Challenge

Instead of fearing rejection, try aiming for a set number of rejections each year. Some writers even make it a goal to collect one hundred rejections. This reframes the goal from getting accepted to simply putting yourself out there. Ironically, writers who take this approach often end up with more acceptances—because they're submitting more work, taking more risks, and growing in the process.

The Compassionate Writer

"Good Writing" is Subjective

The truth is that "good writing" is largely subjective. Personally, I gravitate toward writing that tells a story—something with a clear beginning, middle, and end. I tend to prefer work that is grammatically correct, with paragraphs that each communicate a clear idea. I also appreciate varied sentence lengths, thoughtful punctuation, and clarity of expression. That's what I generally consider "good writing."

But not every journal, publisher, or editor shares that view. I've seen published pieces that ignore conventional grammar or skip punctuation entirely. I've read brilliant work made up of a single, sprawling sentence that stretches for pages. There is no single formula and no one definition of what "good writing" must look like.

I've had writers tell me that they submitted a piece to one journal and received harsh, even insulting, feedback. And then that same piece went on to win a prize—at a respected, competitive publication. What does that tell us? That taste matters. Timing matters. Audience matters. And none of it is entirely within your control.

So what can you control? Your craft. Your voice. Your resilience. The way you respond to feedback. The decision to keep writing—even when the gatekeepers say "no." Subjectivity is not a weakness of the literary world—it's part of its beauty. It means there's room for every kind of story, voice, and vision. The trick is to find where yours belongs.

Anne E. Beall, PhD

Responding Emotionally to Rejection

Rejection is never easy, but how you respond to it can make all the difference. Allow yourself to feel the disappointment—be frustrated, be sad—but don't linger in those emotions for too long. Acknowledge the feelings, then take a step forward.

If you're receiving encouraging rejections, take it as a sign that you're getting closer. Most importantly, remember that one *yes* outweighs a hundred *no's*. You don't need approval from everyone—just the right agent, editor, or publisher who believes in your work.

Sometimes, the issue isn't your writing—it's the match. A well-crafted piece can still be rejected if it doesn't align with a publication's tone, themes, or current needs. One of the most effective ways to respond to rejection is to better understand the places you're submitting to. A little research can go a long way—and might help you find a better home for your work.

Start by reading recent and archived issues of the journals or magazines you're targeting to get a sense of the kinds of pieces they tend to publish. If you're submitting to a publisher, look at the books they've released in the past few years to see if your manuscript aligns with their list. For agents, use tools like QueryTracker to find those who represent your genre and to track your submissions. To dig deeper, visit agency websites to learn more about their clients and recent sales. Understanding what each market values will help you submit more strategically.

Duotrope offers a searchable database of literary markets, with filters by genre, style, response time, and acceptance rates—giving you insight into how competitive a market is. Many listings also include interviews with editors and links to recent publications, which are helpful for understanding what they're looking for. Matching your work to the right outlet isn't just about improving your odds, it's about finding the readers who are most likely to connect with what you've written.

The Real Treasure

Many writers, including Elizabeth Gilbert and Anne Lamott, have said that publishing is overrated and that the real treasure is the writing itself. So if you're chasing that pot of gold at the end of the rainbow, don't forget to admire the beautiful arc of colors right in front of you.

Not all your words will end up published. In fact, probably only a fraction will ever make it into print. For some writers, it might be a very small fraction. But is publishing truly the reason we write?

I know I write to make sense of the world, to understand myself and the people around me—and because, at the end of the day, I love writing. Otherwise, I wouldn't do it. And that is the real treasure. Getting published is wonderful, of course. But the true reward is often the journey, not the destination.

Self-Publishing Versus Traditional Publishing

Many writers begin with the idea that traditional publishing is the only legitimate path to literary success. But that perspective is increasingly outdated. I believe self-publishing is a valid and often empowering alternative. In fact, some highly successful self-published books have eventually been picked up by traditional publishers—who may have rejected them at first.

That said, self-publishing comes with significant responsibilities. If you choose this route, you need to approach it with professionalism. That means hiring a skilled copyeditor to polish your manuscript, using beta readers to gather feedback, investing in a professionally designed cover, and ensuring your book is properly formatted for both print and digital platforms. And then there's marketing—lots of it. Publishing the book is just the beginning; you'll need to promote it consistently if you want readers to find it.

Hybrid publishing is another option. Reputable hybrid publishers offer a middle ground, often providing services like editing, cover design, and formatting as part of their packages. This can lighten the load, but you still need a strong manuscript—and you will be responsible for most of the marketing and all of the cost.

So, as you reflect on the sting of rejection, consider what truly matters to you. How much control do you want over the process? How much work are you willing to do? I've seen writers thrive in traditional publishing, and I've seen others succeed by forging their own path. There is no one-size-fits-all answer. You need to decide what's best for you and your writing.

The following exercises are designed to help you navigate the disappointment of rejection.

Exercise: The Kindest Response

Write yourself a letter as if you were comforting a fellow writer who just got rejected. What would you say to them? Now, read that letter as if it were written to you. Take this out the next time you get a rejection.

The Compassionate Writer

Exercise: The Next Step Plan

For a specific rejection that hits you hard, write down:

- What you learned, if anything.
- One action you can take next (revise? submit elsewhere? start a new project?).
- One reason you're still proud of this piece.

This keeps the focus on growth rather than self-doubt.

Writing Prompts

Processing the Emotions of Rejection

- Describe the moment you received a rejection that really stung. What did it feel like in your body? What did your inner critic say? What did you need your inner voice to say instead?
- List three things the rejection made you question—and then write why those things are still true about you as a writer.
- Write about what rejection meant to you when you first started writing. Has that meaning changed? Should it?

Reframing Rejection as Growth

- Write about receiving a rejection that doesn't cause you to spiral. What do you do instead?
- Describe a rejection you now see as a turning point. What came after it that wouldn't have happened otherwise?
- Write a metaphor for rejection. Is it a locked door? A pruning? A redirect? Let the image shape the piece.

Building Resilience

- Write a pep talk to your future self before submitting something you care deeply about. Remind yourself of your courage.
- Create a "rejection ritual." What symbolic act will you perform after receiving a no? Write about what it would look and feel like.

Reclaiming Your Voice After a "No"

- Write a scene where your most rejected piece finds its perfect audience. Who reads it? How do they respond?
- Write about a time when a rejection was secretly a blessing. You thought you failed, but something better was waiting.

Guided Visualization: The Magical Elevator

Find a quiet space where you won't be disturbed. Take a deep breath in… and out.

Feel the air expand in your lungs, filling you with a sense of calmness. Hold your breath for a moment, then slowly exhale, releasing any tension in your shoulders, jaw, and hands. Let yourself settle into stillness. Now, continue breathing deeply. Inhale… hold… and exhale. Let each breath draw you further into the present. There is nowhere else you need to be—just here, in this moment.

Now, imagine yourself standing inside a sleek, golden elevator. The walls shimmer and you know you're in a magical place. The doors are closed, and in front of you, a single panel of buttons stretches upward. Each button represents a floor of your writing journey.

The Compassionate Writer

The elevator hums gently as you press the first button. With a soft chime, the doors slide open. You step onto the first floor and find yourself in a grand library, the air thick with the scent of old books and leather-bound volumes. Towering shelves stretch toward the ceiling, and at the center of the room, a younger version of yourself sits hunched over a book, eyes wide with admiration. This is where it all began.

You see your past self enchanted by the idea of being a writer, imagining authors as effortless geniuses whose words flowed like magic. You once believed that writing was all about inspiration striking like lightning, and that the best writers never struggled.

You smile at this version of yourself, filled with gratitude for their excitement, their belief, and their courage to dream—even if they didn't yet understand the work that lay ahead.

You step back into the elevator. It's time to move up to another floor.

The doors slide open, and you see a prior version of yourself early in your writing life. You are in a familiar place—maybe sitting at a table or desk. Papers are scattered across the surface, some crumpled in frustration, others filled with half-finished sentences.

You remember the mix of emotions—the thrill of creating something from nothing, the hesitation of wondering, *Is this any good?* You see an old notebook or a computer screen, your first attempts still alive on the page. Not perfect. But real. Your past self doesn't know it yet, but this is the moment they truly became a writer.

The elevator doors beckon you back inside. You step in and press the next button.

When the doors slide open, you find a prior version of yourself getting your first feedback on your writing. Maybe it was a friend or family member, writing group, mentor, or teacher. It's one of the first times you shared your writing with others. You remember the pounding in your chest, the way your hands fidgeted as you waited to hear what they thought.

Maybe you remember several moments when you received feedback. You see someone pointing out weaknesses, suggesting changes. Some of their words are encouraging. Others are hard to hear.

You watch this version of yourself. You see the mixture of hope and disappointment in your eyes. And you remember: this was the moment you began to understand that writing involved getting feedback and growing. It taught you to see your work with new eyes and to listen.

You step back into the elevator and push the button for the next floor.

This time, the doors open into a vast, quiet room where hundreds of letters float in the air. Some are crisp and freshly printed; others are old, their ink slightly faded. They hover gently, whispering familiar words:

"We regret to inform you…"

"Not the right fit at this time…"

"Thank you for submitting, but…"

You walk through the space, touching a few letters, remembering the sting they once carried. But as you step back, you realize that each rejection means you tried. Each one proved you had the courage to put yourself out there. And some of these letters—the ones with some encouragement—remind you that you were closer than you thought.

The elevator waits. It is time to go to a new floor.

The next floor opens into a room filled with stacks of papers, glowing screens, and bookshelves labeled Draft 1, Draft 2, 3, 4, 5... This is the heart of writing life—the place where real writers are made.

You see yourself here, poring over pages, rewriting and revising, cutting lines you once loved. You once thought writing was about getting it perfect the first time. Now, you understand it is about getting it right through revision.

You realize that this room has no exit—because revision is never truly finished. There will always be another draft, another way to improve. And that is not failure. That is mastery.

You board the elevator and rise to the next floor. This time, the doors open onto a floor with a desk and a single letter resting on it. You step forward, recognizing it instantly.

"We are pleased to inform you..."

Your first acceptance. The moment an editor, a publisher, or a reader recognized the value of your work. Maybe this time has already come, or maybe it still lies ahead. Either way, feel the joy of having someone value your work.

And yet, you know this isn't the end. The elevator doors remain open, waiting for you. You step inside once more.

The final floor is unlike the others. As the doors slide open, you step into a room with no roof—just an endless sky above, filled with floating pages. These are stories you haven't written yet, ideas still waiting to take form. You reach out and touch one. The moment your fingers graze the page, words begin to appear—not written by the past, but by the future. This is where you're going.

You step back into the elevator one last time. The elevator gently descends, bringing you back to your present moment. You take a deep breath in… and out.

You are still writing. You are still moving forward. And that is all you need to do.

*

Keep Submitting, Keep Writing

Rejection is part of a writer's life. The only way to avoid it is to stop submitting—and *that* is where real failure lies. Every "no" brings you one step closer to a "yes." Every rejection is proof that you were brave enough to put your work into the world.

Be kind to yourself. Take the lesson and then—submit again.

Conclusion: The Compassionate Writer's Journey

"Be kind, for everyone you meet is fighting a hard battle." — Ian MacLaren (often misattributed to Plato)

You began this journey wanting to explore how compassion could deepen your writing. Along the way, you've discovered that compassion is more than just a technique—it's a transformative force that shapes how you approach yourself, your characters, your readers, and the world. From silencing your inner critic to telling vulnerable truths, from creating multidimensional characters to building a supportive writing community, compassion touches every part of the writing process.

In my own writing, I've come to realize that I have a story—and it's worth telling. Like many writers, I've struggled with that persistent inner critic, the voice that tells me I'm not a "real writer," that urges me to quit. But over time, I've learned to work with that voice, to listen when it has something useful to say, without letting it stop me. I've also discovered that the moments I once hid from—the ones filled with vulnerability and emotion—are often the richest sources of story.

I used to plunge into those difficult moments headfirst, reliving the pain. Now, I try to see the larger narrative behind them. That shift requires compassion—for myself, and for others. It's been the biggest transformation in my writing life, and it didn't happen overnight. I used to see the world in absolutes: villain and victim, good and bad. But now, I recognize the complexity in everyone, including myself.

Compassion has helped me look at my family and myself through a different lens. It's no longer just about what happened, but about why—and what I can learn from it. I've written about conflict, about hurt I've endured, and the harm I've caused. And in doing so, writing has become a source of healing for me.

That said, writing is still hard. Rejection is hard. Feedback is hard. It's painful when your work doesn't land, when you labor over something and it feels like it goes nowhere. This, too, is where compassion comes in—and perhaps it's the hardest place to practice it. As I've improved as a writer, I've also had to grapple with the challenge of getting my voice heard in the places that matter most to me. And so, I keep learning. I keep showing up. I keep practicing patience and compassion.

That's what writing has given me, over time. And that's what I hope it gives you, too.

Compassion is a Lifelong Practice

The compassion we practice as writers doesn't stay confined to the page—it becomes a way of seeing, relating, and living. In many ways, the habits you cultivate through writing—kindness toward yourself, empathy for others, and a willingness to embrace vulnerability—are the same practices that enrich your relationships and your life as a whole.

Compassion in writing isn't something you master. It's something you return to—again and again. There will be days when writing feels effortless, and days when it feels impossible. Some drafts will flow; others will feel stuck. Some feedback will uplift you, and some will sting. Through it all, compassion can be your anchor—reminding you why you write and gently guiding you back to the joy of storytelling.

As you move forward in your writing journey, remember:

- Your voice matters. No one else can tell the story you're here to tell.
- Imperfection is part of the process. Every writer starts with messy drafts. Growth happens in the revisions.
- Connection is your gift. When you write with compassion, you offer readers a chance to feel seen, understood, and less alone.

The world needs your stories. It needs your voice, your vulnerability, and your willingness to explore the truths you have discovered.

Reflection Exercise: How Far You've Come

Pause for a moment and reflect on your journey through this book. What has changed?

- Do you see your inner critic differently than you did before?
- Have you learned to approach your work with more kindness and curiosity?
- What fears have loosened their grip?
- What truths have you uncovered about yourself as a writer?

Every step you've taken—every exercise, every realization, every page you've written—has brought you closer to a writing practice rooted in clarity, connection, and authenticity.

A Final Exercise: Your Writing Manifesto

Before you close this book, take a moment to write your own mission statement as a compassionate writer. What principles will guide your writing process? What affirmations can you refer to when you're feeling low?

Example principles:

- "I will approach myself with kindness, even when I feel stuck."
- "I will write with honesty, even when it feels vulnerable."
- "I will treat my characters as fully human, with flaws and strengths."

Example affirmations:

- "I have a story to tell that is important."
- "I'm improving and getting better at my craft."
- "I am a writer."

Keep your manifesto in a journal, on a sticky note, or somewhere you'll see it often. It will remind you of the writer you are becoming.

Guided Visualization: The Writer's Lighthouse

Take a deep breath in… and let it out slowly. Again, inhale deeply, filling your lungs with air… then exhale, releasing any lingering doubt or hesitation. Breathe in again… and out.

Now, imagine yourself standing on a path of smooth, golden sand stretching toward the horizon. The air is crisp and fresh, carrying the scent of salt and the sound of waves meeting the shore. A warm breeze brushes against your skin.

The Compassionate Writer

You begin walking along the sand. Your steps feel light and effortless. Ahead, rising against the sky, stands a tall white lighthouse with candy-cane stripes. The light at its peak glows steadily, guiding not only ships at sea—but also storytellers searching for their way.

It has been waiting for you.

You walk toward the lighthouse. When you arrive, you place your hand on the worn brass handle of the wooden door. The metal is warm beneath your touch, heated by the sun. With a gentle push, the door creaks open, revealing a winding stone staircase that spirals upward toward the light. Lanterns hang along the curved walls, casting a golden glow.

You begin to climb. At the top, you find a small but inviting room. It's larger than you imagined. You step inside, and it feels like a sanctuary. Small windows overlook the ocean, and there's a quiet warmth within—a sense that you can stay here as long as you like.

Curved shelves line the walls, overflowing with books. Some are the great works of history. Others have titles that flicker and shift, as if waiting to be written. A few lie open, their pages blank and humming with possibility. Others glow softly, already filled with words that have found their way into the world, waiting for the right reader, the right moment.

At the center of the room, a large wooden desk stands ready, its surface smooth from years of creation. Resting on it is a book with a worn navy cover. You walk over and run your fingers along its soft, weathered pages. The ink seems to shift—like it's been waiting for you to engage with it.

You turn a page, and a question appears, written in elegant script: "What do you most want to say through your writing?" Sit with this question. Let the answer rise naturally.

When you feel ready, the page shifts, revealing a second question: "What promise will you make to yourself as a writer?" Let the answer come in its own time.

You notice the windows have opened, letting in fresh sea air. The sky outside is brighter now. The world is waiting for your words. You take one last look around this space, knowing you can return here whenever you need to.

You descend the stairs and step outside. The ocean stretches wide before you, vast and endless—just like the stories within you. You take a deep breath, filling your lungs with the scent of the beach around you.

Then, with renewed purpose, you walk forward—carrying the wisdom of the lighthouse with you.

Acknowledgements

This project has been a long time in the making. Even when I wasn't writing, I was thinking about it—talking it through with fellow authors, revisiting ideas, reworking chapters in my head. I'm sure some of them thought the book would appear any day, but as it turns out, it took a while.

One thing I know for certain: no great book is created in isolation. This one certainly wasn't. If it holds any inspiration, insight, or beauty, much of that comes from the thoughtful feedback I received from so many generous writers.

I am deeply thankful to Megan Baxter, who read every single chapter of this book and whose thoughtful, insightful feedback reshaped several chapters in meaningful ways. Her ability to see the bigger picture was essential to the book's development, and I'm not sure this work would be what it is today without her.

I'm especially grateful to Marcia Harrison for her insightful notes on the fiction chapter. Jill Quist offered encouraging feedback on the emotional journey section—her enthusiasm meant more than she knows. Both of these women have been a deep source of inspiration to me.

Eleanor Vincent graciously reviewed the chapter on healing and shared her experience writing *Swimming with Maya*, offering a powerful perspective on grief and transformation. Her thoughts about writing about the loss of her daughter enriched that chapter tremendously.

Chris Wilkins provided thoughtful feedback on the chapters about vulnerability and the inner critic. His suggestion to explore the role of trust in silencing that inner voice added an important layer of depth.

I also want to thank the members of my Evanston Writers Workshop Critique Group for their patience and valuable critiques across many chapters. Steven Fuller, Boris Glick, Sharon Heller, Sherrie Lowly, Wendy Parman, and John Wolfgram each pointed out things I hadn't seen, prompting meaningful revisions throughout the book.

To the Chicago Story Press Critique Group—thank you for your insights, especially on the Memoir chapter, which evolved significantly thanks to your feedback. Pat Adelizzi, Randi Schalet, Kathryn O'Day, Paolina Milana, and Emma Johnson—your support meant the world to me. I hold deep admiration and respect for each of you.

And to Off Campus Writers' Workshop—thank you for being the supportive writing community I've always longed for. I'm especially grateful to Ana da Silva, Paula Mikrut, Kelly Q. Anderson, Judy Panko Reis, and Tara Maher for creating such a wonderful group.

As always, a sincere thanks to Atiq Ahmed for turning my rough ideas into such beautiful covers. Your talent is incredible, and it's been a great pleasure working with you for all these years.

Thank you also to Ragdale for hosting a beautiful retreat where this manuscript reached its final form. The energy there was palpable—I can't imagine a more fitting place to finish a book on compassionate writing.

Sources

Ahmed, S. J., & Güss, C. D. (2022). An analysis of writer's block: Causes and solutions. *Creativity Research Journal, 34*(3), 339–354. https://doi.org/10.1080/10400419.2022.2031436

Angelou, M. (1969). *I know why the caged bird sings*. Random House.

Atwood. M. (1985) *The Handmaid's Tale*. McClelland and Stewart.

Austen, J. (2002). *Pride and prejudice*. Penguin Classics.

Baumeister, R. F., Bratslavsky, E., Finkenauer, C., & Vohs, K. D. (2001). Bad is stronger than good. *Review of General Psychology, 5*(4), 323–370. https://doi.org/10.1037/1089-2680.5.4.323

Baxter, M. (2024). Wild Creativity: Breaking the Rules to Build a Creative Life. Brevity Blog. https://brevity.wordpress.com/?s=wild+creativity

Beall, A. E. (2023). The Inheritance of Truth. *Grande Dame Literary Journal*. https://www.grandedameliterary.com/post/the-inheritance-of-truth

Beall, A. E. (2023, June 7). Glimpses. *Minerva Rising Press*. https://minervarising.com/glimpses-by-anne-e-beall/

Beall, A. E. (2023, September 21). In Her Coat: Echoes of Life. *You Might Need to Hear This Literary Journal*. https://tomato-plantain-mjnh.squarespace.com/stories/in-her-coat

Beall, A. E. (2024). *Embracing self-compassion: Meditation journeys for self-kindness*. Independently published.

Brontë, C. (2006). *Jane Eyre*. Penguin Classics.

Didion, J. (2005). *The year of magical thinking*. Alfred A. Knopf.
Dweck, C. S. (2006). *Mindset: The new psychology of success*. Random House.
Fitzgerald, F. S. (1925). *The great Gatsby*. Scribner.
Gay, R. (2017). *Hunger: A memoir of (my) body*. Harper.
Gilbert, E. (2015). *Big magic: Creative living beyond fear*. Riverhead Books.
Goldberg, N. (1986). *Writing down the bones*. Shambhala Publications.
Ishiguro, K. (1990). *The remains of the day*. Vintage.
Karr, M. (1995). *The liar's club*. Viking Adult.
Lamott, A. (1995). *Bird by bird: Some instructions on writing and life*. Anchor Books.
Laymon, K. (2020). *How to slowly kill yourself and others in America: Essays*. Scribner.
Lee, H. (1960). *To kill a mockingbird*. J. B. Lippincott & Co.
Lewis, C. S. (2025). *The Lion, the Witch and the Wardrobe*. HarperCollins
McEwan, I. (2001). *Atonement*. Jonathan Cape.
Macrae, C. N., Milne, A. B., & Bodenhausen, G. V. (1994). Stereotypes as energy-saving devices: A peek inside the cognitive toolbox. *Journal of Personality and Social Psychology, 66*(1), 37–47. https://doi.org/10.1037/0022-3514.66.1.37
Merton, R. K. (1948). *The self-fulfilling prophecy*. The Antioch Review, 8(2), 193–210. https://doi.org/10.2307/4609267
Mezulis, A. H., Abramson, L. Y., Hyde, J. S., & Hankin, B. L. (2004). Is There a Universal Positivity Bias in Attributions? A Meta-Analytic Review of Individual, Developmental,

and Cultural Differences in the Self-Serving Attributional Bias. *Psychological Bulletin, 130*(5), 711–747. https://doi.org/10.1037/0033-2909.130.5.711

Mohr, T. (2015). *Playing Big: Practical Wisdom for Women Who Want to Speak Up, Create, and Lead*. Avery.

Morrison, T. (1987). *Beloved*. Alfred A. Knopf.

Neff, K. D. (2003). Self-compassion: An alternative conceptualization of a healthy attitude toward oneself. *Self and Identity, 2*(2), 85–101. https://doi.org/10.1080/15298860309032

Neff, K. D. (2015). *Self-compassion: The proven power of being kind to yourself*. William Morrow Paperbacks.

Neuman, S. (2011). 'Three Cups Of Tea' Author In Hot Water Over Alleged Fabrications. NPR-WBEZ Radio. https://www.npr.org/sections/thetwo-way/2011/04/18/135508982/three-cups-of-tea-author-in-hot-water-over-alleged-fabrications

Nisbett, R. E., Caputo, C., Legant, P., & Marecek, J. (1973). *Behavior as seen by the actor and as seen by the observer.* Journal of Personality and Social Psychology, 27(2), 154–164. https://doi.org/10.1037/h0034779

Ng, C. (2015). *Everything I Never Told You*. Penguin Books

Nickerson, R. S. (1998). Confirmation bias: A ubiquitous phenomenon in many guises. *Review of General Psychology, 2*(2), 175–220. https://doi.org/10.1037/1089-2680.2.2.175

Pennebaker, J. W., & Smyth, J. M. (2016). *Opening up by writing it down: How expressive writing improves health and eases emotional pain* (3rd ed.). Guilford Press.

Poets & Writers (2007). *Turcotte Family Settles With Burroughs, St. Martin's in Running With Scissors Suit.* https://www.pw.org/content/turcotte_family_settles_burroughs_st_martin039s_running_scissors_suit

Salinger, J. D. (1951). *The catcher in the rye.* Little, Brown and Company.

Smoking Gun, The (2006). *A Million Little Lies: Exposing James Frey's Fiction Addiction.* https://www.thesmokinggun.com/documents/celebrity/million-little-lies

Steinbeck, J. (1939). *The grapes of wrath.* Viking Press.

Strayed, C. (2012). *Tiny beautiful things: Advice from Dear Sugar.* Vintage.

Strayed, C. (2013). *Wild: From lost to found on the Pacific Crest Trail.* Vintage.

Tajfel, H., & Turner, J. C. (1979). An integrative theory of intergroup conflict. In W. G. Austin, & S. Worchel (Eds.), *The social psychology of intergroup relations* (pp. 33-37). Monterey, CA: Brooks/Cole.

Vincent, E. (2013). *Swimming with Maya: A mother's story.* Dream of Things.

Vuong, O. (2019). *On Earth we're briefly gorgeous.* Penguin.

Walls, J. (2005). *The glass castle.* Scribner.

Ward, J. (2014). *Men We Reaped: A Memoir.* Bloomsbury USA

Weidener, S. (2010). *Again in a heartbeat: A memoir of love, loss, and dating again.* Independently published.

Westover, T. (2022) *Educated: A Memoir.* Random House Trade Paperbacks

Zusak, M. (2006). *The book thief.* Alfred A. Knopf.

About the Author

Anne E. Beall is an award-winning author and social psychologist who writes about the emotional undercurrents that shape our lives. Her books explore the psychology of relationships—between lovers, family members, friends, and pets who think they're in charge.

She's written eight nonfiction books, including *Cinderella Didn't Live Happily Ever After* and *Only Prince Charming Gets to Break the Rules*, which reveal the hidden messages inside classic fairy tales. Her work has appeared in *People Magazine*, the *Chicago Tribune*, *Toronto Sun*, NPR, NBC, and WGN.

Anne is the founder and editor of *Chicago Story Press Literary Journal*, which publishes true stories that invite readers to see something in a new light. She holds a Ph.D. in social psychology from Yale—so yes, she can absolutely over-analyze your childhood.

She lives in Chicago, where she writes, edits, walks a lot, and tries to convince other people that winter isn't really that long in the Midwest.

She is tremendously grateful to the many people who read her writing

www.ingramcontent.com/pod-product-compliance
Lightning Source LLC
Chambersburg PA
CBHW020455030426
42337CB00011B/120